Dreams and Illusions of Astrology

Michel Gauquelin

Published by Prometheus books
1203 Kensington Avenue
Buffalo, NY 14215

Copyright © 1979 by Michel Gauquelin

Library of Congress Catalog Card Number 78-68134
ISBN 0-87975-099-5

Contents

Foreword

As an astronomer, I am often asked about the relation between astronomy and astrology: Astronomy is the science that deals with celestial bodies and the laws that govern them. Astrology is concerned with an alleged influence of those bodies on human affairs.

Earliest man must have noticed some of the regularity in the motions in the heavens, and to the extent that he speculated on the significance of those motions to his own life, that speculation could be regarded as astrology. But the astrology that is widely practiced today had its roots in Babylonia less than four thousand years ago, and was developed to its present highly complex form by the Greeks scarcely twenty centuries ago. It is, in short, a belief in a magical correspondence between the gods of the pantheistic religion of antiquity and the planets that are named for those gods.

As recently as during the Renaissance, practically all intellectuals believed in astrology; major universities even had chairs in the subject. But in the three and a half centuries after Kepler's discovery of the laws of planetary motion, objective science learned that the planets and stars are physical bodies, made of the same kinds of atoms as we are, and gradually science learned much about the nature of those celestial bodies. More important, it learned the specific laws that govern their behavior—those same laws that dictate the actions of things here on earth. With this new understanding of the physical universe, natural scientists, and those aware of their findings, turned away from the ancient superstition of astrology, and scientists no longer take it seriously.

Yet, astrology is far from dead. In fact, its adherents are growing in number. According to my own polls, about a third of the people in the United States have a rather firm belief in astrology, and at least 90 percent consider themselves "open minded" on the question of its validity.

I think a major reason for the widespread acceptance of astrology is that the true nature of modern science is becoming less understandable to the layman. As the frontier of knowledge is pushed forward, science has become more and more complex, and scientists themselves have perforce become increasingly specialized. Every new subbranch of science develops its own jargon, and each of these new languages is simply incomprehensible to those not trained in it—even to scientists of other disciplines. But without fully understanding science, the public is made fully aware of the new technologies made possible by its findings. To most people, new technical marvels seem almost to be miracles; many have become so used to these miracles that they are prepared to believe anything. Who can blame them? For how is the average person to know that *the Pauli exclusion principle, electron degeneracy,* and *magnetosphere* are part of the language one can read in an *Astrophysical Journal* paper treating pulsars, while *trine, direction, cusp,* and *ascendant* are part of the language of astrology?

Modern astrological charlatans have been quick to seize this opportunity to cloak ancient astrology in the trappings of science and present it *as* a science. They have even taken up the use of the computer, itself a sort of symbol of modern technology. In the United States today there are about ten thousand professional astrologers. They are not all fakes—many are sincere (albeit deluded) believers—but they all make their livings by selling their wares to tens of millions of paying clients.

Astrology has an extremely wide forum. More than two thousand American newspapers carry daily astrology columns. Hundreds of magazines print astrological advice and display advertisements for horoscopes and analyses; many periodicals are devoted entirely to astrology. Extensive bulk mailings offer computer-generated horoscopes and advice for a small fee. The average neighborhood bookstore has dozens of astrology books on its shelves (but probably none on astronomy!). Many radio and television stations broadcast daily astrological announcements, and astrologers are frequent guests on talk and panel shows. Glasses, ashtrays, jewelry, T-shirts, and souvenirs of all kinds feature astrological symbols.

Scientists, on the other hand, have been remiss in recent decades in educating the public about the true nature of their own work. Admittedly it is difficult. Scientists are generally employed full-time in their laboratories or by their universities. Theirs is not a profit-making business, and they have no occasion to advertise for clients. They do not have easy access to the media; a typical astronomer would have no idea how to go about getting on a television program to explain the latest evidence concerning the expanding universe. Anyway, potential scientists are selected for training on the basis of their talent for mathematics and research, and only rarely is this ability coupled with that of a showman. Thus, most scientists are not particularly gifted in explaining their work to the lay public in lucid, elementary, and meaningful terms.

Does the modern obsession with astrology pose a threat, or is it a harmless recreation? In any event it costs the American public tens of millions of dollars per year. Clients follow vast amounts of "astro-psychological" advice of dubious value, and even medical astrology (horoscopic diagnosis of illnesses) is still practiced. Many legislators and government officials seek astrological advice before deciding votes or hiring employees. Numerous bills to accredit schools of astrology and license astrologers have appeared before state legislatures. Most important, in a democratic society of growing complexity and reliance on technology, citizens are robbed of the objectivity they need to make rational decisions essential to their survival.

That is why I am delighted that Michel Gauquelin's book, *Dreams and Illusions of Astrology*, has been released in this English translation. For decades Dr. Gauquelin and his wife have been doing research on birth patterns and planetary configurations. In the course of their work they have had occasion to become extremely well informed about astrology. In this book, Dr. Gauquelin is speaking to the layman, and he describes what astrology is, where it came from, how it works, and its scientific basis (or lack thereof). The account is very lucid and authoritative. I can assure the reader that he will find the pages to follow clear, entertaining, and highly informative. This book is must reading for everyone interested in or curious about astrology.

The final chapter, however, deviates from a discussion of traditional astrology and warrants special mention. There Dr. Gauquelin describes briefly his and his wife's investigation of a possible correlation between times of birth and planetary configurations. The Gauquelins believe they have demonstrated that successful people in various professions have been born with certain planets having just risen or culminated more (or less) often than would be predicted by chance. They have also presented evidence that there is a weak hereditary factor in the planetary configurations at birth. The Gauquelins point out that their findings have nothing to do with classical astrology, and are even contradictory to its predictions. Rather, they suggest that the effects they observe may be related to solar activity, somehow modulated by the motions of the planets in such a way as to trigger the births of certain individuals.

To be honest, I am highly skeptical of the Gauquelins' findings and of their hypothesis. The main reason is that I cannot imagine a mechanism whereby the effect can be produced. However, I do not *know* that the effect is not there; my skepticism cannot be considered close-mindedness, anymore than a gullible acceptance of astrology should be regarded as open-mindedness. If the planetary effects suggested by the Gauquelins *are* real, then their discovery is of profound importance. Consequently, I think the Gauquelins' evidence, based on a great mass of data collected over many years, deserves to be checked out.

It appears now that it is being checked out, and I am delighted to say that the Gauquelins are cooperating fully, and that they demand the most thorough and rigorous objectivity. They are, by the way, absolutely charming people, who are diligent, dedicated, and completely sincere. I find it hard to believe that they will prove to be correct in their conclusions, but if they *are*, I shall join in their exaltation, for the results would constitute a new and exciting frontier of science. And new science comes only from the hard work and the forward-looking, hard-headed objectivity the Gauquelins insist upon—not from dreamy excursions into the superstitious past, to wallow in the ancient murk of the occult.

George O. Abell
Professor of Astronomy
University of California, Los Angeles

Preface

This book was first published in France several years ago. Its main object is to inform the reader about the commercial use and abuse of public gullibility by popular astrologers and their vast horoscope business. For this purpose, I think the book is still useful today, perhaps even more than before. If I were to rewrite this book now, I would modify very few details in the chapters that I consider the most significant—those devoted to the psychosociology of astrology, from old-fashioned fortune tellers to commercial computer horoscopes. The scientific critique also remains valid. Nevertheless, I have to note that in recent years the number and the quality of people who are seriously trying to discover possible proofs for astrological dogmas have been increasing. These people, who come both from astrological circles and from outside of them, must not be put, of course, in the same category as the charlatans and the quacks of popular astrology. They deserve consideration, but I must confess that I still remain unconvinced by the alleged proofs of astrology presented by this new generation of authors. (A scientific examination of some of these alleged proofs can be found elsewhere in the technical reports that I have published.)

The last chapter of this book, "Cosmic Influence," presents the statistical inquiries I have carried out for twenty years, with the collaboration of my wife Françoise, into the relationship between the planets and human personality. This chapter may surprise the scientific reader, though our positive observations do not justify the current use of horoscopes. Essentially, I have nothing to change in this chapter either; but, of course, since it was written, we have continued to explore our field of research. The interested reader may find our most recent results described in the publications of our *Laboratoire d'Etude des Relations entre Rythmes Cosmiques et Psychophysiologiques.* I wish also to mention the increasing interest of the scientific community in testing our observations, particularly in the United States, where a large debate has taken place during the past few years in *The Humanist* magazine. This debate is continuing with tests carried out by *The Committee for the Scientific Investigation of Claims of the Paranormal* concerning whether there is a possible correlation between the position of Mars and the birth of U.S. sports champions. Whatever the conclusions of this committee, it is clear that neither their observations nor ours would in any way present arguments for those who are using astrology for commercial profit.

Michel Gauquelin

Introduction

Despite the progress of scientific knowledge, astrology has maintained itself, unchanging, since the most ancient times. It presents us with animals that we had thought forever vanished but that are discovered one day on some lost continent, spared by evolution and unchanged for millions of years. The fossilized doctrine of astrology is the tyrannosaurus of modern science. It displays its ossified dogmas with the same pride that the Egyptian pyramids show their indestructible silhouettes to busloads of tourists. We cannot question the reality of the pyramids, but what about astrology?

Commercially, there is no doubt that it is quite real. The casting of horoscopes provides a living to thousands of individuals and provides dreams to an infinitely larger number of consumers. In the twentieth century, how is the star business conducted? Who are the astrologers and their clientele? The response to these questions will be our point of departure.

But then, in André Breton's expression, we shall only have described a "prostituted astrology." This is true. Even though it has almost entirely fallen into the hands of charlatans, astrology deserves more than simply an examination of its commercialization. We shall therefore be seeking *another* astrology, a more venerable one that must be treated with more consideration. Let us not forget that through more than fifty centuries of history great minds have reflected upon the mystery of astral influences. The most powerful men on Earth believed in the complex doctrine called *the horoscope*, invented by the Chaldeans and perfected by the Greeks. Even today, it is a popular word. Everyone knows the sign of his birth, but few are aware that the birth sign is but a small part of astrological doctrine. We shall explore this in detail.

This exploration will no doubt perplex the reader. How do astrologers justify astral influence? From the day of our birth are we promised a happy or ominous fate? Are we deprived of free will? We shall confront these theses, from that of universal harmony to that which admits the existence of forces as yet unexplained by science.

We must first of all confront the fundamental problem, a problem that truly puts astrology into question: Is it an illusion or a scientific reality? We shall describe the numerous efforts of researchers to answer this question, from the study of twins to extended statistical investigations of thousands of births. Then the astrologer himself will be judged on his achievements, thanks to an original study based on an objective and almost infallible procedure: the computerized horoscope. This study will be completed by the story of a psychological experiment on the value of the testimony of astrological clientele.

But astrology does not seek to be merely individual. It pretends as well to universality, and believes that it is capable of predicting the course of events and the world's future. The astrology of the world has an illustrious ancestor in the person of Nostradamus. His prophecies have been commented upon down through the centuries. We shall discuss the meeting between Nostradamus and the Nazis; this constitutes one of the most curious and tragic chapters in the posthumous adventures of the prophet. Today, as the spiritual successors of the old master, numerous astrologers read the destiny of the world in planetary cycles. We shall analyze the way in which they continue to exercise their fascination on our contemporaries.

Bouché-Leclerq, one of the greatest historians of astrology, writes: "Astrology is a faith that speaks the language of science, and a science that can only find the justification of its principles in faith." In the final reckoning, our study of the validity of horoscopes will tend to confirm this judgment. But a categorical response to a problem often remains incomplete. Thus in a final chapter we will present experiments whose results seem to indicate that individuals cannot escape certain cosmic influences. What will be in question is the planets, the hour of birth, and professional success. In spite of everything, is this data the hope of a beginning of legitimation for the casters of horoscopes? Not at all, for a more extended study of the phenomena thus placed in evidence shows that it does not correspond to classical horoscopic doctrine, and that only modern scientific techniques permit a valid explanation of it.

CHAPTER 1
Astrologers and their clientele

If it is useful to learn Spanish, if it is desirable to understand Russian, it would seem almost indispensable to be familiar with astrological "language." To be unaware of its vocabulary is to navigate without a compass through the world of the press and literature. It would be indecent to be unable to interpret the meaning of phrases such as: "How does one keep the love of a Virgo?" or "The Virgo mother does not have many children." If these sentences have surprised you, it is only because you read them in English, instead of translating them into "Astrology," as every initiate would have immediately done.

The jargon changes from one country to another but astrological language remains. In this Esperanto of prediction, the world is no longer populated with the good and wicked, with great and small, or with stupid and intelligent individuals. No, the world becomes a menagerie. According to their birth date, husband, wife, and children are transformed into animals that are more or less docile—Aries (the Ram), Taurus (the Bull), or the Scorpion; others that are more or less magical—Sagittarius (a centaur) or Capricorn (a fish-tailed goat); and even more fortunate if they do not become a scale (Libra) or a jug (Aquarius). And thanks to the zodiac, this fantastic little world is filled with its moods, its loves, its hates, its luck, and its misfortune. Mrs. Pisces has married Mr. Cancer (a crab), for

5

water signs make a good couple. But, because she is a Scorpio, Mr. Cancer gets along poorly with his mother-in-law; and the Scorpio, you see, is not absolutely reliable. A crab prefers to back away from a scorpion.

An evening of astrology

How does one penetrate the secrets of this language? Nothing is achieved without effort! You have to work at it, study, and attend lectures. Let us go to an astrological meeting. If you are American, it can take place in New York, Chicago, or Denver. But if you are not, it can also be in London, Paris, Rome, or Berlin—even in Calcutta.

Let us set the scene: a room for three hundred people is already full and buzzing. On a small stage in front are two blackboards, each displaying a flamboyant zodiac. An immense violet circle is suspended above, and on it, in gold, is a superb sign of the zodiac, the sign of Pisces: this is March and today's meeting is dedicated to this sign. Almost everyone is a Pisces, and they have come to hear a lecture on their horoscope. Let us translate: the room is filled with people born between February 20 and March 20, born, therefore, under the sign of Pisces.

From the moment we enter we are offered enticing brochures:

Always a new program, sensational and never before published. Astrology, Science, Art . . . and Humor! An analysis of the fate of each sign of the Zodiac. On today's program: PISCES. Horoscopes of members of the audience: health, character, sentimental and marital destiny. . . . Answers to that always popular question: Who should I marry? The program will include as well the works of popular composers and singers, all of course, natives of Pisces.

In the room the Pisces wait and converse with one another: in "Astrology," of course. In the first row, two elderly ladies are carrying on an animated discussion. One has on an out-of-fashion hat, and brandishes a cellophane wrapped "chart of the heavens" covered with cabalistic signs; she tries to inculcate into another, up to her nose in her camel's hair coat, the rudiments of her science: "No, no! That's not your Ascendant. This is the Second House and here is the First, and *there* is the Accendant. And here, do you see where your Sun is?"

"..."

"No, the Sun isn't the First House! The Houses are marked in black and the Solar Houses are in red. The Second House is your personality. . . ."

"Oh I don't understand anything," signs the other, putting on her bifocals. "Now, is that the House of friends, in Pisces?"

"No, no! The House of friends is the Eleventh. You see, it's marked! And there's Neptune, the master of Pisces. It doesn't look good. . . ."

"Now that's for sure! I would have liked to have a good marriage, like some I've seen . . . like my mother and father, for example. . . . Well, I didn't."

"It's because of your Saturn!"

In the back of the room, half hidden by a large pillar, two couples of young Pisces are carrying on outrageously.

A quick consultation

But suddenly there is silence: the master has just entered. And just as suddenly the chattering little Pisces become . . . as quiet as mice. The lecturer-astrologer is in a dinner jacket. He is one of the great men of the profession, and one of the most well known. He is tall, about fifty, slightly corpulent, and very much at ease. From the first moment, he has the audience in the palm of his hand. He glances rapidly around the room which is full to overflowing: "Congratulations ladies and gentlemen. We have always known that Pisces were punctual!" (There is a murmur of approval in the room.)

There are a few banally astrological words of introduction, and the program begins with the alert notes of an overture by Rossini, a Pisces, of course.

As the final notes are sounding, the room explodes with a violent and sudden tumult: a multitude of voices begins to cry out dates and numbers, transforming for a moment the atmosphere of the room into that of a stock exchange at the closing bell. But it is something completely different. Everyone cries out his birthday, knowing that the master will choose the one with the loudest voice, giving a free horoscope in front of the honored assembly. In the end, it is a rather elegant woman with the voice of a stevedore who wins: "March 7, 1908, at 3 P.M."

Having noted the date, the astrologer begins to construct the woman's map of the heavens on the blackboard, consulting a large book filled with numbers. As the construction goes on, he comments on the horoscope: "Ah, Madame, you are a Pisces, of course, but your Ascendant is in Leo. You are a Pisces in the heart, but a Leo by character. . . ."

"Now that's strange," a distinguished, elderly gentleman murmurs to his blond neighbor.

"The moon is at 29 degrees of Taurus: this is a thrifty Pisces. . . . Mercury is at 2 degrees of Pisces, but retrograde: you bet at the races, Madame? . . . or at least you ought to. . . . Mars is at the 9th degree of Taurus, and Jupiter is in conjunction with Venus. . . . Ah, ha! Saturn is at 28 degrees of Pisces, in the Eleventh House: here is something that contradicts a little what I said about betting on the races; Saturn is the planet of restriction. . . . Uranus in Capricorn trines Mars. . . . Humm. . . in any case, Madame is a psychic! Do you have any children, Madame?"

"I have a 25-year-old son."

"Well, Madame, if your son is not married yet, I can tell you that in a month, Venus will be in your lucky region for this young man. According to your astral chart, this Venus could very well be a wealthy heiress. Advise him to not let her get away!"

There are a few more predictions, and then the astrologer goes into a more general discussion of health, destiny, and the lucky days for Pisces. During the intermission, there is music—"Lakme, Your Sweet Gaze Is Hidden," by Leo Delibes, followed by Chopin's "Tristesse," (both Pisces)—soft drinks, and the sale of booklets on *Your Sign* for one dollar which are quickly snapped up. There is shoving, elbowing, and feet are stepped on.

When the program begins again, the astrologer speaks brilliantly on the romantic destiny of Pisces, "the tenderest, the most gifted, but unfortunately also the most lymphatic of the signs." Finally, he lists the famous people born under this sign, explaining that, despite appearances, people such as Rossini, Pius XII, Caruso, Einstein, Joliot-Curie, and Victor Hugo were "all Pisces, Pisces above all!"

The audience is attentive. Many close their eyes in order to better understand. Some take notes. There is even someone who records the master's words on a tape recorder.

In all, the master will have spoken more than two hours by the clock, holding the undivided attention of his audience, now making them laugh, now (although less frequently) throwing out a threatening prediction, making the atmosphere a little heavier for an instant. But the uneasiness is short-lived; the master is a good fellow, and most often there is laughter.

When the program is over and the audience has begun to flow towards the door, they are rocked by the sonorous waves of a largo by Handel (like them, a Pisces). Thus for those who two hours earlier knew little about it, astrology has taken on a new resonance: amusement, fear, admiration, or distrust? In any case, there is no one who is indifferent.

Perhaps the person will have been surprised. But he is wrong: this routine program was classic and banal. Throughout the world, thousands of astrological programs similar to this one take place every week. Each one always draws a larger and more impressed audience, an audience that is not, as we are sometimes led to believe, just composed of the ignorant, the gullible, and misfits. Far from it! The audience is everyone: blue and white collar workers, small businessmen, fashionable women, housekeepers, actresses, teachers, dressmakers, and retired people. They all come to drink at the inexhaustible source of this mysterious, eternal, and miraculous science. . . .

A flowering business

The French dictionary *Larousse* defines astrology as "the art of predicting the events of an individual's life through interpretation of the planets." In the 1930 edition, *Larousse* added, "In our time, this superstition has long since disappeared." But in the 1964 edition, this final sentence has been omitted. And this is easily understood, for this ancient knowledge, as old as humanity itself, is in perfect health.

The regeneration of astrology began between the two World Wars, and first of all in English-speaking countries. Later, it reached the Continent. France has not been spared. At the present time, astrology is found everywhere, on every streetcorner. Newspapers are filled with horoscopes, and even the least astrological of magazines are adorned with revealing titles: *Constellation, Zodiac, Planet,* and *Galaxy*. Advertisements for candy use the signs of the zodiac to arouse the imagination. Even when we weigh ourselves on coin-operated scales, we receive a card that has a short astral prediction on the other side.

Furthermore, there are horoscopes for every budget: the prices vary between fifty cents (the price of a postage stamp) and 500 dollars (for this price you receive a veritable illuminated chart, in the style of the Middle Ages).

In 1954, Francois Le Lionnais published some astonishing figures: there are 30,000 offices of occult and astrological consultation in France. The total of expenditures for magic is about $450 million per year. Well over a million dollars per day for this adventure— much more than is spent on scientific research! With the money the French spend in a year for predictions of the future, it is said that over 600 miles of highway could be built. According to the estimates of the Paris police, in Paris alone there are 3,460 offices of astral prediction that have declared to the Bureau of Taxation an income of more than $5 million since 1935, not to mention what they did not declare. Not knowing how to classify this profession, the Bureau of Taxation finally put astrologers in the category of "information bureaus"! And of all the money spent on fortune tellers, seers, tea leaf and card readers, astrologers seem to receive the lion's share.

We find the same phenomenon in the United States. In an article devoted to a famous American astrologer, *Time* (March 21, 1969) declares: "The number of Americans who find astrology amusing or fascinating deserves serious study; it is the source of a substitute faith, and has transformed a minority into a social phenomenon." And the following figures are given: there are 10,000 professional and 575,000 amateur astrologers in the United States. For his part, in a study published in 1954, Le Lionnais stated that there are over twenty magazines dealing solely with astrology, and their circulation exceeds 500,000 copies. For publicity, one of them uses astrological parades where twelve girls in assorted swimming suits in the colors of the twelve signs of the zodiac march to the sound of enticing music. Even in 1943, more than 2,000 newspapers carried an astrological column, and a poll indicated that "five million Americans followed the directives of astrologers, spending more than $200 million per year to discover their destiny."

The situation has not changed, except perhaps to increase. In the United States, radio greatly aided the audacity of charlatans. "After a series of talks, Miss A. received 150,000 requests for horoscopes in three months; and another charlatan, offering a 'complete solar horoscope' for one dollar, received 30,000 one dollar bills in the mail."[1] Once they were banished from American radio, they found refuge in Mexican radio, giving their return address as General Delivery. In 1943, astrology almost became a legalized profession in California: Proposition 1793 passed through several committees before being defeated by a narrow margin. Analogous figures can be found in Germany, Italy, and England. In fact, astrology has vigorously invaded all five continents, and with astonishing success.

In India, the final page of the daily papers is entirely devoted to astrology. Good parents in that country publish classified announcements that extol the merits of their son or daughter of marrying age, including a horoscope that contains the astrological genealogy of the whole family.

In the East, important marriages never take place without the advice of an astrologer. The hour and date of Soraya's marriage to the Shah of Iran were set by the court astrologer, in order for it to be under the most favorable auspices. (This astrologer must have had problems keeping his job later!) For their marriage in 1963, the Prince of Sikkim (a province in northern India) and his American wife had to wait a whole year. According to custom, the astrologers were asked to choose a favorable date—which delayed the ceremony a year.

In Japan, the country of low-priced industrialization, astrological publications make available more than eight million *Koyomi*, pocket horoscopes in several colors and within reach of every budget.[2] In a recent article in the *New Yorker*, the great novelist Han Suyin relates that throughout Asia, astrology is considered to be an ultramodern science. And this is why "there is no problem that Far Eastern astrology cannot solve."

At all levels of society

Astrology has infiltrated society at all levels, and even the most brilliant minds have been unable to resist its fascination. Particularly since the Second World War, politics has flirted with astrology, and we shall examine later the role that the prophecies of Nostradamus have played in this closed field.

For several decades, literature, as well, has become interested in astrology. André Breton's *Surrealist Manifesto* was launched on an exceptional planetary configuration. Henrich Maria Remarque, author of *All Quiet on the Western Front*, insisted to his publisher that his book *The Arch of Triumph* (later made into a film starring Ingrid Bergman and Charles Boyer) appear on a day set by an astrologer.[3] Very recently, speaking on the attraction of astrology on financial and entertainment circles, an American journalist stated, "Wall Street and Hollywood are the Babylons of the twentieth century!" A great number of movie stars believe in astrology and have regular consultations with astrologers. And far from hiding the fact, they are proud of it. Among the well-known devotees of this art, *Paris-Match* lists Michele Morgan, (born on February 29), Mylene Demongeot, Roger Vadim. . . . It is the same for the artists of high fashion: Coco Chanel believes in the influence of the stars. Poiret, the great designer of the Roaring Twenties, never presented a new line without asking Max Jacob, the poet, if the day was favorable.

According to Paul Couderc, in 1940 Will Hays, the American film producer, was ready to make twelve films on astrology. Having learned of the project however, certain scientific organizations did everything they could to discourage him. The films were never produced, but it was the war that prevented the projects of Will Hays.

The world of business is perhaps even more under the influence of astral rules than the world of the theater. Billionaire J. P. Morgan, one of the titans of American capitalism, had a personal astrologer, a certain Evangeline Adams. This lady, on trial for the illegal practice of fortune telling, supposedly made so convincing a horoscope for the judge's son that she was immediately acquitted.

In Marseille, an "astrologer-numerologist" sells to businessmen "astro-suggestive predictions," a complete set costing five hundred dollars if one is to believe the red and yellow announcement, covered with esoteric designs, sent "free and without obligation." For this modest sum, the customer has the right to the "financial anatomy and tendencies of the stock markets of Paris and New York one year in advance."

Astrology is often no more than one way among many to easily earn a living. One of the most wealthy and most popular astrologers in the United States, the Great Zolar, began as a clothing salesman. One day, he financed an astrology program on the radio. When the star of the show failed to show up, he took over himself. His success was immediate, and he began a new career. It is said that he sees no clients in person, but rather specializes in astrology by mail, applying elementary astrological formulas and using the most modern IBM cards in order to make more money. But we shall return to computerized horoscopes later.

Thus everything leads to astrology. But astrology can also lead to everything. If the Great Zolar began as a clothing salesman, the Fakir Birman, the most famous French astrologer before World War II, finished his career by selling new models of ladies' lingerie, one model of girdle being the most successful. Charles Fossez, alias the Fakir Birman, owed his success in the astral science to a lawsuit—which he won, it must be noted—brought against him by the husband of a client who had been deceived by that husband. This happened in 1932. Until its closing in 1939, the Fakir's astrological service grew steadily to gigantic proportions.[4] In 1936, the Fakir had an advertising budget of one and a half million dollars, received 1,400 letters daily, sent out 3,500 letters, and spent $140,000 annually on postage stamps. His exact profit was never known, but was estimated to be about one million dollars or so; he declared only $9,000 to the Bureau of Taxation. On March 22, 1939, his career as a fakir came to an abrupt end when he was convicted of fraud. It was then that he began (with the same efficient methods) his business in ladies' undergarments. After having published his memoirs—*My Memories and My Secrets*—in 1946, the Fakir, a sick man, committed suicide in 1950.

People and astrology

But what does the man in the street think about this plethora of predictions that is unleashed on him? Recently, many surveys have been undertaken by psychologists and sociologists in many countries. Their first assertion is: from one country to another, there is little variation in people's opinion of astrology. A study conducted in Germany between 1950 and 1956 by the German Demoscopic Institute, under the direction of Professor Hans Bender of the University of Friburg-Brisgau showed that of Germans over eighteen years old, 30 percent believed that the heavenly bodies had an influence on life; that 20 percent, without necessarily believing in it, did not think that such an influence was inconceivable; and that 7 percent had had a personal horoscope cast. More recently, there was a poll conducted in 1963 by the French Institute of Public Opinion (IFOP) at the request of an evening newspaper (according to Evelyne Sullerot, this poll increased the circulation of the paper by 30,000). Fifty-eight percent of those questioned knew their astrological sign, 53 percent read their horoscope in the newspaper, and 38 percent would have liked to have a personal horoscope cast for them. These high percentages are explained by the fact that many consider astrology to be a recognized science. Every day, observatories receive requests for horoscopes. For forty-three people out of a hundred, the astrologer is a scientist who does not make mistakes; 37 percent believe that their personality corresponds perfectly to the sign under which they were born; and 23 percent state that the predictions of horoscopes are remarkably accurate.[5]

In November and December of 1967, the attitudes of the French toward astrology were again studied. The study was of a nationally representative sample of 6,000 men and women between the ages of eighteen and sixty-five. It is thanks to *Irès Marketing*, who conducted this study, that we are able to reproduce here the essentials of the responses to the question, "Who are the 'clientele' that give astrology such striking success?"[6] Fifty percent of the men and 70 percent of the women—about twenty million people—state that they read astrological columns in newspapers and magazines, even if only on occasion. From these results, if the regular readers are only 10 percent or 20 percent of the total, the size of the audience is impressive. The profile of this audience is notable for its youth: beginning with 71 percent of the readers of horoscopes being between eighteen and twenty-five, the percentages regularly and significantly decrease with older age groups. For those over fifty-five, the percentage of those who read horoscopes is below 50 percent. This raises a new paradox: The curiosity in the achievements of this ancestral and traditional science is more widespread among the young than among their seniors.

Interest in astrological columns is manifested almost as much among the well-to-do as in the more modest levels of society. Only farmers are relatively recalcitrant: while more than 60 percent of all other categories read horoscopes, the figure falls to 44 percent among farmers. It is true, however, that the latter are significantly less exposed to the different media, and this certainly at least partially explains the difference. This is the opinion of Jacques Maitre, a sociologist with the French National Center for Scientific Research (CNRS) who has recently examined the phenomenon of astrology: for him it is a "symptom attached to modern industrial society," and furthermore, "astrology has largely extended beyond the boundaries of the other techniques of mass communication.[7]

After noting that 4 percent of the women and 2 percent of the men questioned stated that at least once, they have purchased magazines especially dedicated to astrology, the researchers remark that the clientele of astrologers is more often feminine than masculine: "Whether it is a question of astrologers or other fortune tellers, the rate of visit is three times higher for women than for men." It is also noted that the astrologers' clientele is relatively better off financially and tends to live in or around Paris. The conclusion of the study is: "There are twenty million more or less regular readers, four million who consult more or less seriously, and one million more or less curious buyers: such are, in general, the limits of this paradoxical market." It is easily understood why astrologers have profits that are, shall we say, astronomical.

For its part, the IFOP poll of 1963 sought to trace the profile of an average client. One finds it to be a woman, still young (twenty-five to thirty-five years old), with a high school education, and with a satisfactory income. This lady is most interested in her personal future, and admits giving little importance to that of others. But she is also curious about predictions on world politics and imminent catastrophes. Her interest in the three principal domains of astrology—love, health, and money—depend on her preoccupations of the moment.

Daily astrology

For astrology, there is nothing that is irreducible: even those who "do not believe at all" in horoscopes are familiar with them, and feed their hostility by carefully reading the astrological column in their newspaper.

In thousands of offices, a secret weekly ritual takes place on the day that the weekly women's magazines appear on the newstands. In an office somewhat removed from the supervisor's desk, the ladies circle about the owner of the magazine who presides over the meeting, the astrological page spread across her knees. Each one in turn comes to learn about her immediate future. Each sentence elicits an echo for these ladies. They know each other's little intrigues in detail, and transcribe every pronouncement of the horoscope into the context of their daily lives: "Sagittarius: Beware of people wearing uniforms." The office breaks out laughing, for the most recent arrival, born under than sign, has been flirting with a policeman!

Astrology is unrivaled as a topic of conversation. Thus, there is no truly successful get-together without it. Every organized and up-to-date hostess knows that as soon as the conversation begins to falter, she need only mention the subject to get things going again.

There are families blessed by the stars, who have the good fortune to possess a specialist more or less conversant with this great art. If he is just slightly loquacious (and he usually is), the strange little cousin or retired great-uncle is the life of the family get-together, particularly when the occasion is somewhat taxing, like Thanksgiving or Grandmother's eighty-fifth birthday. But he also excels at marriages, showers, baptisms, and first communions.

"and you, Susie, . . . when were you born? Scorpio? Ha, ha, ha!" (Everyone laughs.) "Well, that doesn't surprise me at all. . . ."

And now everyone, drawn by the first mysterious revelations, begs the family astrologer to tell their horoscope:

"Tell me, Uncle Victor, . . . when will you cast my astral chart?"

"Does my horoscope have bad or good aspects?"

The astrologer uncle shrugs his shoulders and raises his arms towards the heavens: "What do you want me to do? I don't have the time. A horoscope takes a long time to cast. . . ."

But no one is discouraged, and he lets them all think that one day, each member of the family will be able to have his future unveiled. This little blackmail assures him the maximum of respect . . . and invitations!

A remedy for solitude

No one is unaffected by interest shown in him; everyone likes, first of all, to be told about his personality, then his little problems, and finally what new and exciting things will happen to him in the near future. It can even be the distant future, as long as it is "sensational": a young mother will not be at all surprised if it is predicted that her chubby little baby will be president one day. A veritable avidity to know the future takes hold of those who have the good fortune to find themselves in the presence of someone who claims to possess its secret.

Our Western civilization is not at all miserly with its benefits: we are offered in abundance what we need to eat, to wear, and to amuse ourselves. From this, a new need appears, no less demanding than the others: the need to be understood and admired by those around us. But this new need remains most often unsatisfied. The rhythm of modern life is too fast for us to find an attentive and receptive ear to listen. The problem is not serious for he who is happy in his family and in his work, and whose health leaves nothing to be desired. Such a person glances laughingly over the daily horoscope in his newspaper along with a quick consultation with a friend who is an amateur astrologist. Occasionally, he might even buy a little book about the signs of the zodiac.

But not everyone is happy: far from it! All those who feel misunderstood and lost in the big city—or out in the country—find that for a little money given to the astrologer, they finally become the center of interest. It is the same for those who meet with serious difficulties in life, those shattered by problems that they find themselves unable to resolve alone. The sorrow of love, grave illness, bankruptcy, the duplicity of their friends. . . . All this leads to the person who seems to control forces that are at once scientific and supernormal: to the astrologer. The letters received by the professionals of the stars show it clearly; their clients are above all unhappy and dissatisfied people, whom they serve as helpful guides or as a means of escape.

Dear Sir:
    At the present time I am working very hard to make a go of it in a label printing shop, and the results fall far short of my efforts. Faced with my deceptions and my discouragement, my husband advised me to write to you. We hope that it will be possible to have a horoscope. I would even be willing to study

some other trade or become an apprentice if I were certain it would be profitable. For the moment I have only finished grade school, and I would like some guarantee before making any great sacrifices. Here is my birth date. I hope that a lucky star was there at that time. . . .

Advertising

But how do you find good addresses? Without further delay, let us go behind the scenes of astrology. Who are the astrologers? What are their tricks? Are there good and bad astrologers?

Hope is sold in this profession like people sell drugs or household appliances: and most of all, it is sold through advertising, which the fortune tellers know inside out. To the same end, they use slogans, brochures, signs, classified ads, whether free or paid, and so on. "Bring your troubles to him." This is the slogan used by the precursor of the popularization of astrology, the Fakir Birman, in 1935. Since then, this type of lucky idea has multiplied. Here are a few examples taken at random from astrological announcements:

> You can live the life you want: IT'S NEVER TOO LATE. There are indications from transiting influences in the year ahead upon your very own birthdate that can help you get exactly what you want.

Brochures are passed out in the street, or are sent by mail. They usually are based on a friendly eclecticism:

> "Don't wait"
> "Your horoscope from day to day:
> Your Health—Your Love Life"
> "Your Subconscious—Your Destiny"
> "How You Can Win the Daily Double"

But it is newspaper and magazine ads that are the cornerstone of all client recruiting. Most often, they are found in magazines specializing in the occult sciences, in ladies' magazines, or even in periodicals that successfully offer dreams at a low price.

Imagination and a wide variety of talents are included in ads, but certainly not modesty. This can be seen in a short little ad, evidently aimed at the less fortunate:

Prof. Z . . .: Hind. astrol., int. rep. Abs. dep. & disc. by rt. mail. Remar., health, wealth, ed., etc. sat. guar. Date of b. $5.

At the other extreme are the gigantic advertisements, those of the more successful in the profession. Madame F. publishes no less than full-page ads, which include a large photograph of her. She is in no way an amateur, since she is: "Certified Astrologer and Graphologist, Certified Psychologist-counselor"; besides astrology, she practices "Egyptian Tarot, Chiromancia, and Radiathesia." She usually resides in Paris, but we are told that she accepts consultations in Cannes every year during the international film festival. In addition, foreigners will be happy to note that she is a distinguished linguist: "English spoken, Man spricht Deutsch, Si parla Italiano," promises the advertisement. Finally, it is to be noted that her references are at the level of her prices: *"Who's Who,"* the Cercle Militaire, the *New York Herald Tribune.*

It is clear that she is, as her advertisement says, "the astrological seer of both the Parisian and international elite." As for her slogan, it is: "I bring happiness," decorated with a little four-leaf clover. The advertising of her colleagues pales a little compared to hers.

For the impenitent lover of the track, we can recommend: "Astrology for the Daily Double, Astro-scientific methods, Proven big profits. Daily Double-Trifecta. Send your birth date. Five combinations for one dollar." Clearly, one cannot do better than that!

Astrologers: The true and the false

Finally, and especially, there is the horoscope. The horoscope, the center of all hopes and dreams, is composed of different parts of the celestial arch, which of course must be correctly assembled: zodiac, aspects, planets, houses, and so on. The astrologer must know how to construct a complicated chart of the "Heavens at Birth." (Or at least he ought to know how!)

From this point of view, would you like to know how to distinguish a "true" astrologer from a "false" one? Basically, it is that the true astrologer knows the astronomical correspondences of the astrological terms he uses. For example, he knows that the "Dragon's Tail" in a horoscope represents the point of intersection between the plane of lunar orbit and that of the ecliptic. For his part, the false astrologer is sadly quiet about such questions. But in general, he gets out of difficulty by asserting that, for him, the horoscope is no more than one of the complements of his abilities as a psychic!

In spite of appearances, all of this is very serious, and has been the basis of court cases. According to Marcel Boll, "A certain Gaspard Toudon who practiced astrology (as Professor 'Blue Star') was indicted for fraud in July 1939. It was established that during the year he had spent over $27,000 on postage stamps, and had a net income of $80,000 using the title of astrologer." But he was forced to admit before the court that he knew nothing about this science. Nonetheless he believed in it to the point of having his horoscopes made up by "serious astrologers." As such, there were extenuating circumstances in his favor. But in its decision, the court condemned him, stigmatizing him with the term "false astrologer."[8]

And how do the "true astrologers" go about their business? Large tomes written and published by astronomers for their own use furnish specifications as to the positions of the stars in the heavens for each day and for each hour of the day, for the past as well as for the present and future. Astronomers have spent many years on this work. But the astrologer uses it to establish the heavens at birth, not needing to pay any more attention than he would when consulting a train schedule. But once the chart has been established, it still must be interpreted. And this is where the "true astrologers" are triumphant. From this astro-photographic slide of the subject's birth, they are able to draw out the "quintessence." Examining the zodiac with their practiced gaze, they will tell you if the group of your planets—Mercury, Venus, Mars, Jupiter, and so on—moving from sign to sign, presents favorable or unfavorable configurations in their relationships. On your chart, they will write the good aspects in blue, like so many good grades; as for the bad aspects, they will put crosses on your astrological circle, like on a bad student's homework. You thus have a poor grade on the composition of Fortune and Destiny.

The horoscope may be complicated at will. We shall return in more detail to this in Chapter Three.

The Modest Ones

Whether true or false, astrologers are like bureaucrats: they can be found at all levels. Let us meet them, from the bottom rung to the top of the ladder.

The foot-soldiers of astrology are most often of the feminine sex. They are found in rural areas and are the least fortunate of the profession. Unable to offer their clientele the Scenic Tour or the Enchanted Labyrinth, these ladies must be content with receiving their clients in their modest living rooms, between a stuffed owl and a crystal ball, their hands placed upon a dusty oriental tablecloth. These enchantresses perpetuate the tradition of the country fair, far removed from those who sacrifice today to speed and electricity. These gypsy medium-astrologer-seers predict the future according to their inspiration of the moment, and charge a modest fee that varies greatly according to the demeanor of the client. Occasionally, becoming lazy and making some sacrifice to modern technology, some of these ladies do no more than keep an eye on a machine that delivers horoscopes printed in advance to those who put a coin in the slot that corresponds to their birthday. Their clientele is composed for the most part of naïve young couples and groups of joking adolescents that decide to buy a low-priced horoscope for a lark.

Above this "infantry" in gypsy costumes, we find what might be called the "recruiting sergeants." They are something found in large department stores. In one of them, a truculent fortune teller is installed between the nylons and the artificial flowers. The customers wait in line to receive their consultation.

"A tortuous, violent, yet fecund sign, governed by the planet Mars. . . . And now, here is a free envelope containing your destiny." A button is pressed, and up steps the next client, who has been waiting in line. "Your firm and vigorous appearance indicates good health. But the dangerous sign of Scorpio makes you subject to infections and illness, in particular a tendency to overindulgence in drink." There is the glibness of barkers and street hawkers, and the docility of the audience is instructive.[9]

The proprietors of department stores seem quite satisfied with their astrologers. It seems that they appreciably increase business. There is nothing surprising in this. On the contrary, every newspaper knows very well that the elimination of the astrological column brings about an astonishing drop in circulation.

... And the others

All this is not very serious; let us now consider the practitioners who have reached the rank of "officers" in the astrological army. There is today a kind of conflict in their midst, a battle between the young turks and the old guard. In order to better understand the sides in this debate, let us examine what separates these two astrological worlds.

First the old. They have titles of nobility, and their names have a pleasing resonance: Professor Anthenor, Ely Starr, Omar Kahn, and Samy Sarla. All of them wear turbans and goatees; they have a piercing gaze (at least in their photographs). In their brochures, they emphasize their "Oriental birth"; they are, so they say, "real Hindus," which of course implies that there are "false Hindus"! Others in their crowd, more modest, admit that they are only vulgar Westerners like you and I. And they emphasize that this fact only makes their discovery of the secrets of the East more meritorious.

This old wave of astrology, still hard at it, usually works by correspondence. It would certainly be uncomfortable to receive clients if they always had to be in a turban and covered with yellow make-up. Moreover, the setting-up of an Oriental decor would demand a substantial investment that not all could afford, particularly at the beginning of their careers. Being of an especially "disincarnated" mentality, these astrologers declare themselves to be "more mystical than mathematical," and for them, the beauties of astrology "are felt more than they are explained" (as Boileau said of La Fontaine). Their "right-wing" mysticism brings down upon them the thunderclaps of the "left-wing" astrologers who, more materialist and more dialectical, claim to explain astrology in a modern way, through waves and rays. But in spite of everything, be assured that the sages of the old wave have their feet firmly on the ground, that they have well-rounded bank accounts, and that they know how to realistically exercise their "sacerdocy."

Setting up shop

Let us examine the way clients are drawn in; it is a well-practiced technique, one proven by traditional astrology. The first act begins with the offer of a free sample:

> YOUR HOROSCOPE FREE: You too, you have a right to happiness! OMEGA, one of the world's greatest astrologers, offers to examine your case and to elaborate your astrological study ABSOLUTELY FREE. You will receive marvelous revelations on your FUTURE, regarding MONEY, LOTTERY, BETTING, HEALTH, LOVE. Write to Omega, ZO Service, Post Office Box . . . Indicate the date of your birth, and enclose a self-addressed stamped envelope.

The client rises to the bait and writes. He then receives, by return mail, a plain envelope (dispatch and discretion!) containing an all-purpose horoscope, the same for everyone, pompously entitled "Partial Horoscope" or even "Beginning of a Complete Horoscope"![10]

It is composed in such a way that it can be sent to men as well as women, and it appears to have been written especially for you, thanks to the latest achievements of the most modern duplicating machines. Here is a lovely example, included by Patrice Boussel in her *Guide des Voyantes*:

Free Predictions

State of the Heavens no. 128B

Examining the astral chart of your birth, although your planet reveals contradictory forces, certain of which eliminate one another, it permits the hope of a noticeable amelioration of your situation. This planet gives a changing personality, sometimes active, daring and audacious, other times fearful, timid, reserved, docile, and calm. [The Magus takes no chances!] This mixture of two absolutely different personalities [in which each client is assured of recognizing himself a little!] will constantly threaten you, and will even separate you from your closest friends. You must be very careful of too many changes that will occur shortly and that will cause you serious problems if you are not careful, bringing sorrow and difficulties that can be avoided. [That is: it is now or never that you must consult me, who alone can conjure away the threat!] Hoping that you will understand that I am unable to tell you more without compensation. . . .[the allusion is discreet!], I cannot advise you too strongly to request immediately a more extended study, if only the two-dollar study, if that is all your budget will permit.

Signed, The Magus B.

The free horoscope, the cornerstone upon which the astrological clientele is constructed, is thus carefully constructed of a blend of compliments and contradictory remarks, of hidden dangers that the client ought to know if he wishes to protect himself. The global horoscope is governed by three general principles:

1. Your character is not understood by your friends.
2. At the present time, your future is threatened.
3. The practical offer, for a limited time, of a paid but more complete horoscope. The client must not delay his response, for he might forget to do it at all. He is offered discounts and premiums for a quick response. Here is one of the responses received by Maurice Colinon in his study.[11]:

My fee for a complete horoscope is ten dollars. If you send your request within three weeks however, it will be done for the exceptional and confidential price of eight dollars. Furthermore, for that amount you will also receive, absolutely free, a marvelous charm of radioactive metal, whose powerful and beneficial force has been carefully and scientifically measured.

The second act: the client responds once to these attractive offers and he must now be brought to the status of a regular customer; for he begins to talk about himself, giving details about his life that will later be given back to him, without his even being aware of it. He will thus be overwhelmed by the wisdom of the astrologer. Henceforth, in the friendly words of one of these Magi "the client and the astrologer will walk the road of life together" (to the profit of the astrologer, to be sure . . .).

But the client does not always respond after having received his free horoscope. He receives a letter that is more threatening, while it offers a reduced price. It is the global letter number two:

I have not found any amelioration in your situation. It is urgent that you know certain facts that seem to be becoming certain in the aspects of your heaven. If I may be direct, it is in your own interest. I would like to believe that your hesitation is only due to the price, however modest, and so, in order to show you how interested I am in your destiny, and joining in the fight against inflation[!], I am willing to make another sacrifice for you, and ask you for only six dollars.[12]

If the client still does not strike the bait, he finally receives a third letter, or a "final warning." It is pathetic to the point of excess:

While looking for a dossier among those that I consider especially interesting, I ran across yours. . . . I thought about discarding it, but my desire to advise you prevented me from doing so without at least warning you. Rather than knowing that you are without friend and guide, I prefer to abandon all personal remuneration and offer you your horoscope for the sum of four dollars.[13]

It can be seen that, at times, the astrological trade is not an easy one, and that for every successful Fakir Birman, there are a great number of Magi that laboriously struggle for tight-fisted clients.

The astrologer in the gray flannel suit

Let us now turn to the new wave: with it, astrology is no longer sold as "preserves" but is freshly picked. The new astrologer does not write to you, but rather receives you in his home. With his shingle on the door, like a doctor, lawyer, or dentist, he has his hours of consultation. And for some of them, it is advisable to make an appointment several days in advance, for their agenda is full.

This new wave rebels against the use of all-purpose, mimeographed horoscopes. Received in chambers, the client is always "personalized." Here, there is piecework rather than mass production. The astrologer is a scientifically distinguished artisan. The attention is felt, and consequently so are the prices.

There is an important point to be noted: this modern astrologer practices his art in a suit. No longer magus or fakir, he presents himself as a scientist, offering a rigorous, exact, and mathematical science. Besides, following the footsteps of the Empress Josephine, who became "more than a queen," the astrologer here becomes "more than an astrologer." He calls himself a cosmo-biologist, an astral-physicist, an astral-psychologist, and so on. It is less picturesque, but how much more serious! Where the magus-astrologer only made predictions, the scientist-cosmo-biologist makes "anticipations," which, it is said, seem not at all the same! He will also explain to you that man's free will still exists, in spite of astral influence: "Astrology foresees the future," writes one of this new breed, "but the view is still obscure [a shame!]; for it is still up to the subject to cause the anticipation to happen or not." Finally, the modern astrologer claims the title of psychologist: he is a doctor of souls as much as he is a doctor of the heavens. We shall examine later the pretentions to the scientific level. For the moment, let us accompany Roland Harari into the office of one of the most famous modern style astrologers, a certain John V., who lives in a middle-class apartment building in a small city. His gestures are serious and measured. His waiting room might be that of a doctor or a lawyer, if there were not a plaque on the wall certifying him to be a "counselor-astrologer." There are no stuffed owls or pointed hats here: rather a global projection, a slide rule, blackboards, filing cabinets, a great many numbers, and a great many drawings. He lets it be known that among his clients are a bishop, three foreign heads of state, a handful of politicians, a professor of medicine in Paris. . . . The latter wrote for advice about his health, addressing him as "My eminent colleague" (According to *Science et Vie*, this letter actually exists).[14]

In November 1962, there was a kind of official consecration of this astrologer: on order from a minister concerned with foreign affairs, four pages were eliminated from the astrological magazine for which he writes, for his predictions "might have been harmful to a foreign head of state." Evidently the minister attached some importance to the prediction.

We enter here the Olympus of the profession, where one can find a few god-astrologers whose number in each country can be counted on your fingers. They are blue-chip stocks. They have written successful books; they have opened schools of astrology and presided over conferences; they are well-known to a certain "enlightened" public; they flirt with intellectuals and poets; and in their clientele are jet-setters, bankers, actors, and government ministers.

Each of these inhabitants of the astrological Olympus has a strong personality. And like the English dandies of the late nineteenth century, their renown in the world is based on an original specialty that they have elaborated for themselves. One is known for holding astrology in one hand and psychoanalysis in the other; another could not explain your horoscope without using her great discovery: "Double Houses"; and all have offered to their readers knowledgable, convincing, and yet varied explanations of the influence of the heavens on our lives. They deserve to be examined.

Newspaper Horoscopes

But we shall examine later the value of these higher astrologer speculations. Let us now pass on to the story of the astrologers of the daily newspapers, a territory that was pioneered after World War I. It is a fertile land where the harvest is almost miraculous. The astrologers of the press attain a renown that is often international. This is the case, for example, of the illustrious F.W. He lives in Rome, but his fame is so great that he was chosen to write the astrological column for a large French magazine.

Who is F.W.? When he was interviewed a few years ago, he was described as about forty, with a gourmet's face, smooth gestures, and a soft voice. F.W. would resemble an affable prelate in a tweed jacket, if it were not for his gaze: strange, at once furtive and incisive, a gaze that looks through the questioner, making him ill at ease.

"Mr. W., you write the astrological column in a large magazine. What are the bases upon which you elaborate the weekly horoscope?"

"I proceed as if I were casting the horoscope of an individual, but I do it for each sign. Besides the traditional calculations, I use a very ancient system of calculation that is Arabic in origin, and I use Chinese astrology as well. When I synthesize all of this, I use my gifts as a seer."[15]

The results of this astrological cocktail can only be remarkable. And it is a prediction that is remarkably widespread as well, since it is to be found in *Elle*, a weekly publication that carries his prediction to some 100,000 ladies born under the same sign!

Outlaws and the mentally ill

Our chart of the astrological world would not be complete if we did not speak about those interlopers, the outright charlatans of this art. They constitute the dregs of the profession. Their cynicism is shocking, and it often prevents them from receiving any tolerance from the judicial system. For it must not be forgotten that in most countries, astrology is against the law. If we open the French Penal Code, for example, we see that it is directly prohibited by Article 479 of the Law of 4/28/1832: "Those whose trade is divining, prognosticating, or explaining dreams shall be punished by a fine of not less than 1,300 and not more than 1,800 Francs"; or Article 480: "Diviners and interpreters of dreams shall be imprisoned for a period of not more than five days."

Today, this law is used especially to fight against those of whom a "serious" Parisian astrologer said: "Sixty percent of these pseudo-astrologers learned astrology in prison; you notice that they all give their address as a post office box! Or else they live in the distant suburbs of Paris, being parolees who are prohibited from residing in the city." They learn from their cellmates that it is a profitable racket: the risks are much less than forgery or armed robbery; and in this trade no one asks for references or for an arrest record—no more than they ask to see the diploma one claims to have. It is for this reason that many well-meaning people are seeking to obtain some kind of official status for competent astrologers, with the intention of getting rid of the others. The problem is in the definition of "the others," for relations between astrologers are not cordial, and they often claim that all the others are charlatans.

Finally, there are the mentally ill, those afflicted with an astrological delirium (or simply delirium). The newspaper astrologers receive long letters from them regularly, and they have great difficulty in responding to such letters.

But the usual clients of astrologers are certainly not always mad; more often, they are people with anxieties, who suffer occasional depression or are simply curious. Their problems are sometimes so complicated that even the most experienced astrologer cannot make head or tails of them. In his *Confessions d'un Astrologue,* the Belgian G. L. Brahy tells of an adventure he had one day. A lady came into his office, "an elderly lady with an austere air." After much difficulty, the astrologer was able to find out that she came to consult with him about an affair of the heart. During a prolonged discussion, he finally discovered the nature of the lady's problem: she was in love with a priest. "Little by little, in monosyllables, she told how she had been taken with her confessor, an understanding man, indulgent towards human weaknesses, with an abundance of self-presence. She related how, from nuance to nuance, she was able to communicate her feelings to the prelate." Brahy adds, "It was extremely difficult for me to be of service to this client, who, having a horror of moralizing, wanted only one thing: to be told that the stars were favorable to her. In fact, perhaps she was hoping that I would offer her a love potion, and advise her to seduce her confessor, bring him to her feet, overflowing with passion and ready to make the final renunciation of his calling."[16] In such situations, the astrologer cannot even appeal to the resources of ancient Rome where the fortune tellers had to predict the future by interpreting the appetite of a sacred chicken. In order to be able to count on a prognostication that would conform to the desires of the populace they did not feed the birds for three days before the ceremony.

Throughout history, religions, morality, and laws have condemned the occult sciences, and astrology was always among the first to be condemned. But in spite of this, astrology is not about to disappear. It will always be our contemporary, reflecting man's desire to know his future and to make it favorable, against storm and high tide. This is the secret of its force and fascination in the century of man-made satellites. But up to now, we have only bitten into the outer layer of this forbidden fruit. Its popular and anecdotic features do not exhaust it. Like the iceberg that only shows one-tenth of its mass, hiding the remainder under water, there is another astrology that is worthy of attention. It is not necessarily composed of a thousand and one adventures of obscure and influential personages that traffic in the destiny of others, using the fascinating attraction of the heavenly bodies. Not at all. It has other claims to glory and nobility. "It is a very great lady, beautiful and come from afar, who seems to me to hold one of the noblest secrets in the world. It is a shame that today a whore is in her place": so said the poet André Breton.

Notes

1. P. Couderc, *Astrologie,* p. 106 (Presses Universitáires de France).

2. *Life,* March 28, 1960.

3. *Paris-Match,* August 13, 1960. *(Paris-Match* is a French magazine modeled after *Life* and *Look.* NT)

4. Patrice Boussel, *Guide des voyantes* (Paris: La Palatine), 26.

5. *France-Soir,* 1/26/63 (a Parisian daily similar in tone to the *New York Daily News* [NT]).

6. *Ireś Marketing:* May 22, 1968, *Les Francais et l'astrologie,* by J.-C. Fuffa.

7. *Adam,* October 1967, p. 19.

8. M. Boll, *L'Occultisme devant la science,* PUF.

9. Boll, *L'Occultisme,* p. 55.

10. Boll, *L'Occultisme,* p. 55.

11. Maurice Colinon, *Les Marchands d'Horoscope:* La Tour Saint-Jacques, #4, 1956.

12. From the letters received by Colinon *(Les Marchands d'Horoscope,* p.6–7).

13. Ibid.

14. *Science et Vie,* January 1963.

15. *France-Soir,* January 31, 1963.

16. Op. Cit. *Flandre-Artois,* 1946.

CHAPTER 2
Roots in the past

The historian Franz Boll writes: "As strange as astrology often seems to modern man, it has nonetheless been one of the spiritual forces common to all mankind for several millenia; its literature can be called worldwide; and it represents perhaps the only domain where East and West, Christians, Moslems, and Buddhists understand one another without difficulty." This is certainly true: astrology is a doctrine that neither has nor ever had borders: it is a planetary belief.

At once humanity's first religion and first science, astrology has assumed a variety of forms. Through the centuries and across the continents, it has also been known under a multiplicity of names and assuming different *fasti*. In Mexico, before the conquest of the New World, the conjunctions of the stars signaled the time for bloody human sacrifices. In ancient Egypt, the lovely star Sirius was particularly venerated, for it had been noticed that it rose with the sun during the season when the life-giving flood of the Nile fertilized the earth, parched by the burning sun. Ever since the most ancient days in China, the emperor was considered to be the center of the world. This "son of heaven" represented the standard for measuring the whole universe. He sacrificed to the stars so that he might be in perfect harmony with them, and he was responsible for astrological predictions. In India, the pilgrims have always come to purify themselves in the sacred Ganges, and their numbers are greatest when certain formations of stars are observed. But it is not our intention here to follow the different avatars of belief in the stars, particularly since they assume forms that are very distant from classical astrology. We have already done this in another work.[1] We will be content here with evoking the origins and development of the most common form of astrology—the doctrine of the horoscope of birth—and the way it has survived up to the present.

Chaldea

More than 4,000 years ago, in the region we call Iraq today, towers were raised in each city: in Uruk, Ur, and later in Babylon (the location of the Tower of Babel described in the Bible). These towers constituted the first observatories of the heavens. For it was in Chaldea that astrology was really born. In spite of their already advanced technical abilities, the Chaldeans lived in magic. Everything around them had the value of a sign that needed to be interpreted: dreams, conduct, and even the manner of sneezing were the ways in which the gods manifested their plans. But more than man, Nature was a kind of pentacle with a multiplicity of manifestations, whose meaning it was essential to penetrate. The strangest was no doubt this "inverted bowl that is called heaven," in which the stars carried on a silent, perpetual ballet. Through patient observation, the Chaldeans discovered that this ballet followed certain rules, which they considered to be magic. The sun, the moon and Venus were the first three gods of the sky to be identified: the Chaldeans called them *Shamash, Sin,* and *Ishtar*. Thanks to the assuiduity of several generations of priest-astrologers, their heavenly paths were determined. Sin, the Moon-god, was an elderly man with a beard of lapis lazuli. The Sun-god Shamash was his son and master of the earth, which he circled in 365 days. Ishtar, the morning star, was the goddess of war, the "brave daughter of Sin," "lady of battle and combat." But " Ishtar, the evening star, is the goddess of love, pleasure and fertility."[2] The priests soon noticed other "wild goats" which, each at is own velocity, followed the same celestial paths as the three great gods: they were the planets Mars, Jupiter, Saturn, and Mercury. The first was given as a kingdom to Nergal, the god of war, the second to Marduk, the king of the gods, the third to the disturbing and morose Ninib, and the last to the wily Nebo. Then, the astrologers divided the "Anou Way," the way of the planets, into twelve regions.

Thus by 419 B.C. the famous signs of the zodiac were born, a fact stated in a cuneiform text that has survived to the present day.

These signs were populated by strange creatures from the Babylonian pantheon: the Scorpion, the Centaur, the horse with a man's torso (Sagittarius), or Capricorn, the aquatic monster with a double being, a goat with the tail of a fish. It is probable that at the beginning, as Van der Waerden has stated, the zodiac was only a calendar, whose twelve signs represented the twelve months.[3] It is then understood why the royal power of the Lion (Leo) was attributed to the burning sun of the month of August. And why, inversely, the three signs of winter are signs dominated by the aquatic element: Capricorn (with its fish tail), Aquarius (whose name is explicit enough in itself) and Pisces, the Fish.

Thus deciphered, the heavens furnished omens. The first astrological pronouncements come from Sargon the Elder (3,000 B.C.). At the beginning, the signs of the heavens were used to predict natural cataclysms and severe weather, something that was later called *meteorological astrology*. Thus, an old cuneiform text states: "If a halo surrounds the Moon-god, the country will be rainy and cloudy." But the field of application was soon enlarged. There arose an interest in the country's fortunes in war, and soon the future of the king was read in the stars, as shown by the questions answered by the priest-astrologers on the cuneiform tablets. Until then, the documents do not mention the date of birth. The tablets laid out the king's questions to the astrologer: "Should this war be undertaken?" "Will the harvest be bountiful?" and so on, something that will later be called *horary astrology*.

But then, around the fifth century B.C., it happens that the documents deciphered by experts speak of a relationship between the position of the "god-lights" at the moment of birth and the destiny of man. Little by little the horoscope, the fundamental doctrine of popular astrology, was formulated. At first, only the king had the right to have a horoscope, and even this one was cast without taking the hour of birth into account. The oldest known horoscope dates from 410 B.C. It is Babylonian and was recently published by A. Sachs. Another dating from 263 B.C., however, is markedly more explicit. It comes from the city of Uruk. Here then, is a portion of it (the ellipses correspond to gaps in the document):

In the 48th year of Selucid, in the month of Adar, the 23rd night, the child is born. On that day the sun was at 13½° of Aries, the moon at 10° of Aquarius, Jupiter in the beginning of Leo, Venus in the house of the sun, and Saturn is in Cancer. Gemini, Aries and Aquarius are in the house of his . . . the months of Ayyar, Ab, Arahsamna . . .[five lines here are unin-

telligible] . . . love . . . wealth will be lacking. . . . His nourishment [will not be sufficient?] for his hunger[?] the wealth he
possessed in his youth [will not last?] In his 36th year he will
become rich. He will live to an advanced age. His wife, that
people . . . in his presence. . . . He will have . . . and wives. He
will find benefits. During a journey for commerce he. . . .⁴

On the whole it is a horoscope that is neither very good nor very
bad.

But when the Chaldean astrologer was carefully elaborating
the destiny of this child born the night of the 23rd day of the month
of Adar in the 48th year of Selucid, it was 70 years after royal
Chaldean astrology had passed the flame to Greek astrology. Since
the conquest of Chaldea in 330 B.C. by Alexander the Great, the
renown of Chaldean astrology was spreading throughout the Med-
iterranean world, from the mysterious sources of the Nile to the
land of the Hittites. Thus "the historian ought not be surprised that
the Greeks succumbed to the charms of the horoscope."

Greece

Although astrology was not born in Greece, its greatest minds did
not wait for the conquest of Chaldea to reflect upon the role played
by the heavenly bodies. Thus, while meditating on the movement of
the planets, Pythagoras, born in Samos around 582 B.C., developed
the famous theory of the Harmony of the Spheres, a philosophical
concept in which the planets were supposed to trace the celestial
route while each one emitted a different musical tone. Plato, born
around 427 B.C. in Athens, and his pupil Aristotle, born in northern
Greece at Stagire in 384 B.C., accepted more or less implicitly the
influence of the stars.

Chaldean astrology was introduced to Greece by the work of a
priest in the temple of Marduk at Babylon, a certain Berosus, who
had come to Cos, the island of Hippocrates. The assimilation of the
Chaldean planetary gods into the gods of the Greek pantheon was
accomplished without great difficulty. But very soon after, new
elements appeared. It was thought that the stars exerted an influence on the destiny of all men. Henceforth, each individual had the
right to a horoscope, and it was no longer a uniquely royal privilege.
The horoscope of birth contained the seed of a child's entire destiny,
like the seed planted in the ground contains in it the virtuality of its
germination, flowering, and ultimate death. Furthermore, careful
to work with precision, the Greek astrologers wanted to know the

hour of birth of their clients. In particular, they strived to determine the sign that rose on the horizon at the moment of birth; the Romans would later designate this the Ascendant (the term is still in use today), but the Greeks called it simply horoscope, whose literal meaning of which is "I look at the hour." Obviously, the meaning of this word has greatly evolved since then.

Since everyone had the right to a horoscope, the Greek astrologers found themselves obliged to complicate the doctrine, in order to obtain a variety of predictions large enough to explain the diversity of human characters and destinies. While for the Chaldeans astrology was still the observation of appearances, for the Greeks, it became a bookish doctrine, where nothing was left to chance.

This was clearly established fifty years ago by a member of the French Institute, Bouché-Leclerq.[5] For their part, Neugebauer and Van Hoesen of Brown University published in 1959 a translation of 180 Greek astrological horoscopes that are still known today (in their monumental work *Greek Horoscopes).*[6] The most valuable sources however, are still the Greek treatises on astrology written at the beginning of our era, which are still extant: works like Manilius' *Astronomicon,* a vast astrological poem of over four thousand lines, composed at the time when Julius Caeser controlled the destiny of the Roman Empire: and the *Tetrabiblos* by Claudius Ptolemy, one of the most famous astronomers in ancient times, a work dating from 140 A.D. To give an idea of Ptolemy's importance, it can be noted that his explanation of the world given in *Almageste,* another of his books, was generally accepted until Copernicus refuted it by declaring that the sun and not the earth, was the center of the universe, fourteen centuries later. This also shows how, for a long time, astrology and astronomy were considered to be complementary sciences.

It is symptomatic that *Astronomicon* and *Tetrabiblos* first saw the light of day at the moment of Roman domination. No doubt these works were compilations of older works, and this is why they are so precious to us. For the history of astrology is one of continual rebirth. Babylon had abandoned astrology to her Greek conquerors, and in turn, the Greeks transmitted their knowledge to their conquerors, the Romans.

The study of these treatises teaches us that Greek astrology already contained all of today's astrology. Since the Greeks, innovations, the "complete horoscope" has not changed: the signs of the zodiac acquired the precise meaning they have today, the theory of astrological "houses," and that of good and bad "aspects" were all invented by the Greeks. It was they that had the idea of calculating precise predictions for an individual's whole life by comparing the birth chart with the ulterior movement of the planets in the heavens (transit, direction, and so forth). In short, Greek doctrine is that of modern astrology. We shall have the occasion to analyze this in a later chapter, but let us now give an overview of the twenty centuries of history that separate the two.

Rome

The names of the planets that we use today are those of the gods of the Roman pantheon: Mercury, the messenger of the gods; Jupiter, the father and master of the gods; Saturn, the dethroned god. That is, we carry on Rome's interest in astrology.

It was introduced by Greek slaves brought in captivity to Rome (from 250–244 B.C.). At first blamed for all the evils that befell the Roman world, the "Circus astrologers," as they were derisively called, nevertheless took on more and more importance. Outside of the traditional soothsayers, there was established, in each village, a group of free-lance fortunetellers, the Chaldeans who came from the East. The "official" soothsayers finally protested, and the astrologers were driven out (by decree of Cornelius Hispallus, in 139 B.C.). But in vain. They definitively established themselves during the Republic (144-39 B.C.). The numerous social upheavals that shook the Roman world during this period were not at all foreign to their success. In an excellent work,[7] Frederick H. Cramer tells the story of two popular agitators, Eunus the Syrian and Athenio the Sicilian. These two men were popular as a result of their predictions. This shows how the fortunetellers and astrologers had progressed in the lower ranks of society. But very soon after, the Roman intelligentsia was won over to the cause of horoscopes, thanks in part to the influence of a great philosopher, the Stoic Posidonius. The Consuls Octavius and Sylla "are two examples of this first generation of Roman aristocrats who admired the reality of astrological predictions," says Cramer, adding that the fact "that political leaders like Julius Caesar, Crassus, and Pompey accepted flattering (although incorrect) horoscopes offered by obsequious astrologers is symptomatic of this new era."

Not everyone in Rome was contaminated by the astrological faith, however. There were a few skeptical thinkers—although more and more rare—who criticized it. Outside of them, this was something new in the history of astrology. Up until then, it had been accepted as self-evident and indubitable. In his famous *De Natura Rerum,* Lucretius, the Epicurean philosopher, opposed astrological fatalism to human free will. Cicero attacked it in the name of reason. In his *De Divinatione,* he lists eight arguments against the futility of horoscopic belief. But his voice went almost unheard. Eventually, the last bastion of skepticism had to capitulate. From the Roman Empire on, astrologers were the privy counselors of the emperors, were close to power, and passed on the post from father to son: it was an obscure but powerful dynasty.[8] "The young emperor Augustus," writes L. MacNiece, "a thoughtful and realistic individual, was so impressed by the glorious future predicted for him by an astrologer named Theogenes that he published the horoscope and had a silver coin minted bearing a likeness of Capricorn, the sign of his birth." Tiberius' favorite was an astrologer named Thrasyllus, who was at the apogee of his influence between 23 and 36 A.D. For all practical purposes, he held the reins of power. His death caused great suffering to the aged Tiberius. Thrasyllus' heir Babilus took his place, continuing in the same capacity for the emperors Claudius and Nero. It was certainly in vain that the poet Juvenal attempted to arouse the clients of the astrologers, in particular, the Roman women. The astrological tide carried everything in its wake.

When Heliogabalus, who was from the East, became an emperor in 218 A.D., he took the name of Sun-god, worshipped at that time in Syria through the symbol of a black conical stone. This stone was transported to Rome "in a solemn procession through the streets of Rome." As Gibbon relates it: "the ground was covered with gold dust; like a gem, the black stone was placed on a chariot drawn by six richly decorated white horses."[9] The adoration of the sun cannot be totally identified with astrology, but it responds to the same aspirations. And there can be no doubt that most astrologers were worshippers of the sun. The old Roman gods no longer interested anyone. "Beginning in the fourth century A.D.," writes Bouché-Leclerq, "a certain faith in astrology became part of common sense, and it was only in excess that it became superstition." For already some time however, astrology had been faced with a rival more dangerous than the auguries and soothsayers of ancient Rome: Christianity.

The star of Bethlehem

When Jesus was born at Bethlehem, a small city in Judea, the wise men, mysteriously alerted to the event, took route in order to adore the Savior. During the night, they were guided along their journey by a star—so says the Bible. What was this celestial apparition?

Some say it was a comet that crossed the heavens at that time. Others—like Kepler, for example—think that it was an extraordinary conjunction of Mars, Jupiter, and Saturn. It is said that the three planets were superimposed in the sky in such a way as to appear to be a giant star, more luminous than all the other heavenly bodies. What is interesting to note is that shortly after, the birth of Christ was associated with "signs from the heavens." As Saint Jerome notes, these wise men were originally just *magi,* three astrologers. This observation embarrasses the Church Fathers. Would not the announcing of Christ's birth by a heavenly sign be a "certificate of veracity presented to astrology by God himself, who must have followed its rules in order to make the message intelligible?" asks Bouché-Leclerq; and he adds, "Saying that God used a star to inform the magi just because they were astrologers does not change the conclusion: they were informed, and therefore they understood heavenly signals!"[10]

In fact, coming from the East like astrology, Christianity penetrated first of all the lower levels of society. Like the astrologers, Christians were persecuted not only because their faith opposed the Roman gods, but because they were troublemakers. But the resemblances stop there: the unavoidable destiny indicated by the heavenly bodies is opposed to the merciful will of the Christian God. In the declining Roman Empire, the seductive astral doctrine soon lost its charm for the great men. When the emperor Constantine converted to Christianity in 333 A.D., astrology was reduced to the rank of a "demonic" practice.

But the astrological seed that had found its way deep into the soul of the people still had to be extricated. This is why Constantine replaced the solar festival of the winter solstice with that of the birth of the Savior. The image is clear: the days that had slowly grown shorter up to that moment began to become longer once again, a prelude to a new springtime. Later, Sunday, the day of the sun, became the "Lord's Day," and the pagan solar-lunar festival of spring became Easter, the celebration of the Resurrection of the Savior at the same time as the resurrection of nature after its Winter sleep. Thus even today, Easter is not on a fixed date but continues to be celebrated on the first full moon of spring.

This systematic undermining was to bear fruit. The generous Christian doctrine replaced the old belief in the heavenly bodies, from which there was no possibility of redemption.

In the Western world, the fall of the Roman Empire into the hands of the barbarians from the north brought the decline of astrology but not that of Christianity. Saint Augustine's role was crucial to this. As the Bishop of Hippone, in North Africa, St. Augustine lived from 354 to 430. In his *Confessions,* Augustine tells of his youthful belief in astrology, and his subsequent reflection on the birth of twins: ". . . for the most part they came out of the womb so near one to another, that the small interval (how much force soever in the nature of things folk may pretend to have) cannot be noted by human observation, or be at all expressed in those figures which the astrologer is to inspect, that he may pronounce truth. Yet they cannot be truth: for looking into the same figures, he must have predicted the same fate for Esau and Jacob, whereas the same happened not to them. Therefore he must speak falsely; or if true then, looking into the same figures, he must give the same answer. Not by art, then, but by chance would he speak truly."[1]

Saint Augustine compares Christian faith to the belief in astrology: "Christian piety, true piety, repels these practices and condemns them. . . . Remember the words of the Lord: 'Now you are healed; sin no more or else fear the worst.' This saving precept is attacked by the astrologers when they say: 'the inevitable cause of sin comes to you from heaven.' or, 'It is Venus, Saturn or Mars that is responsible.' They thus acquit man of all fault—man of flesh, blood, and prideful decay—and place it upon the Creator, He that governs the heavens and the stars. . . ." For a thousand years, the authority of Saint Augustine was not questioned in the Christian West.

Islam and the Middle Ages

At this time, however, astrology did not disappear from the globe. With its religious fatalism that is sometimes so close to astral predestination, the Arab world and Islam in particular, gathered in the heritage that so many peoples had already passed along. This partly astrological fatalism is to be found in Omar Khayyám, the Persian astronomer and poet of the eleventh century who was one of the eight men selected by Malik Shah to revise the calendar:

This inverted bowl that is called heaven
Under which the race of men struggles and dies. . . .
He moves at will the impotent markers
On the chess board of days and nights
Puts them in check, takes them up and puts them away
One after the other, back in their case.[12]

It was especially in Bagdad, the city of the thousand and one nights, that "astrology and astronomy—like Siamese twins—regained their past glory under the patronage of such caliphs as the famous Harum al-Rashid. An observatory (the proof that these studies were serious) was built in Bagdad and used by astrologers like Albumasar."[13] Albumasar was one of the most famous astrologers, and his book, *The Flowers of Astrology*, founded on Greek and Egyptian tradition, was later one of the first books published after the invention of the printing press by Gutenberg. "There is an amusing anecdote about Albumasar," writes Peukert, the astrologer from Bagdad who died in 886. He was the student of a doctor at the court of Persia, and was criticized in public by Alkindi (at the time an important astrologer). He decided to kill this gainsayer. Armed with a dagger, he entered the room where Alkindi was to be found. The astrologer gazed fixedly at the intruder and said: "Art thou not Albumasar of Balkh? Thou shalt be the greatest astrologer of the century, but thou must renounce thy evil design. Throw away thy dagger, sit down and accept my doctrine. Albumasar gave in and became the master's best student."[14]

The greatest minds of the Islamic world were passionate students of astrology. But none of them added much to the doctrine they had inherited: in the Middle Ages, the astrology of the Arabs penetrated Europe by way of Spain. It was a time when Christian faith began to become less intense. This is no doubt why predictions such as those of the famous *Letters from Toledo* exerted such an influence. In 1179, the mystic Juan of Toledo announced that there would be a gathering together of all the planets in Libra in the year 1186: he predicted a universal catastrophe. All Europe was thrown into fear. But in the end, nothing happened.

Three centuries later, another panic was provoked in Europe by astrological predictions. Let us cite Paul Couderc:

"A widely read author of almanacs, Johannes Stoffler, announced in the edition of 1499 that twenty-five years later, in 1524, there would be new terrible floods as a result of numerous planets being in conjunction with a *water* sign. In spite of the resistance of the astronomers, people everywhere were uneasy; messengers were sent to Charles V asking that he designate places of refuge; people sold their houses and furniture and took refuge on ships; and others went insane with fear. In Brandenburg, the Margrave and his court gathered on the Kreuzberg near Berlin to await the terrible event. It goes without saying that February, 1524, was unusually dry."[15]

The Renaissance

Beginning in the sixteenth century—and particularly in Italy—an irresistible current led the great writers to criticize certain intellectual structures that had been ossifying since the Middle Ages. The Greek and Roman civilization was rediscovered; the first printers made available the principal texts of antiquity, thus providing a wealth of extremely rich new ideas that were to give impetus to the development of modern science. Paradoxically, while the great men of the age put astrology in question along with the other sciences, they did not reject it.

Paracelsus (1493–1541), the father of hermetic medicine, elaborated a theory in which in a surprising combination, he associated astrology and the whole of alchemy of his day. For this impetuous theoretician, there is a correspondence between the exterior world—the heavens in particular—and the different parts of the interior world—the human body—with the whole apparatus regulated by a universal principle that he called *Magnale-Magnum* and described as a kind of cosmic magnetism. According to him, a doctor should always consult the heavens before prescribing anything. The principle organs of the human body correspond to the seven planets: the condition of the heart was governed by the sun, the spleen by Saturn, the brain by the moon; Venus governed the kidneys, Jupiter the liver, and Mars the bile. For Paracelsus, alchemy could not be dissociated from astrology. Man was composed of three primordial elements: mercury, salt, and sulphur. According to him, illnesses were caused by a discord among these three elements or by the predominance of one of them. The stars necessarily played an important role in the dosage of medicine to be prescribed.

Another great man of the Renaissance was a famous astrologer, Geronimo Cardano, born in Pavia in 1501 and who died in Rome in 1576. This Italian was at once doctor and mathematician, philosopher and astrologer. Even though he was named doctor of medicine in Padua in 1524, he taught mathematics at Milan. Towards the end of his life he was accepted into the College of Physicians in Rome and was given a pension by the Pope. Cardano was one of the most eminent astrologers of his day but also one of the most unfortunate. His sincerity cannot be doubted, for he insisted on including a dozen of his most monumental errors in his *Geniturarum Exempla*. We shall relate only his adventure with Edward VI, King of England and son of Henry VIII. In 1552, Cardano went to Scotland to care for a prelate. On his return he stopped at the home of Sir John Clerke, the preceptor of young King Edward, then fifteen years old. The pious little prince was in poor health, and Cardano was asked to cast his horoscope; he did so, and gave an exceptionally careful commentary on the document. Jupiter in mid-heaven promised a splendid career; Leo was the ascendant: the gage of a long and happy life. Cardano announced that Edward would lead a normal life up to middle age, but after "fifty-five years, three months and seventeen days he would be afflicted with diverse illnesses. Alas, Edward died the following July, nine months after Cardano's prediction. He was sixteen years old."[16] Cardano was a strange character, and seemed to be subject to fits of insanity: "J. Scaliger and de Thou claim that Cardano, having predicted the date of his death through astrological calculation, allowed himself to die of hunger in order to justify his prediction."[17] But—and this is the constant paradox of the Renaissance—Cardano was an authentic man of science to whom posterity owes much: in mathematics he made numerous algebraic discoveries; and navigators owe him an ingenious method of suspension that, with a special apparatus, permitted the compass of ships to be independent of the movement of the hull.

All of the great astronomers of the period were more or less astrologers. Copernicus gave Rheticus, a dedicated astrologer, the responsibility for publishing (in 1540) his fundamental *De Revolutionibus Orbium Caelestium,* where for the first time he proposed that the sun was at the center of the planets. The Dane Tycho-Brahe (1546–1601), who furnished the world with tables of the planetary positions unparalleled at the time for their precision, also cast many horoscopes, for he believed that the stars influenced character and destiny. But he nonetheless forcefully struggled against charlatans who lived by fraud. The same attitude is found in Johannes Kepler (1571–1630), who discovered the laws of movement for the stars. Einstein wrote that Kepler's thoughts about astrology "show that the inner demon, though conquered and rendered inoffensive, was not however, completely dead." In fact, as MacNiece states, this inner demon "was much more alive than Einstein admits."[18] Kepler professed the whole gamut of attitudes towards astrology, from complete adhesion to systematic denial. The truth is that he refused all the predictive astrology of the almanacs (one would call it today "commercial astrology"). It was for him a lot of "frightful superstition" and "idiotic witchcraft." But he confusedly believed in a new astrology, completely renovated in the way that the astronomers of his time renovated astronomy. "One should only disbelieve idiocies and blasphemy; from the astrologers a useful and healthy wisdom can emerge." He firmly believed in the Pythagorean theory of the harmony of spheres, where each planet emits different notes in its orbit. The fact is that this belief played an important role in his discoveries about the architecture of the universe. And later, great men like Galileo and Newton seemed to never have completely renounced astrology.

But in only referring to Paracelsus, Cardano, and Kepler, we are forgetting a whole other side of Renaissance astrology. Everyday magic ruled throughout Italy. Princes had their astrologer-counselors. Popes did not hesitate to have their horoscopes cast. Astrology was taught in universities, and cities were not built nor marriages performed without the advice of a "planetarist." "What proves the permanence of astrology and the homage paid to it is, among other things, the frescoes of the Schifanoia Palace in Ferrara, where figures are shown respectfully presenting the attributes of the art."[19]

The history of France

If one studies the relationship between astrology and the history of France, it becomes clear that from Robert the Pious to Louis XIV it was in the forefront of royal preoccupations. In his *L'Astrologie populaire*,[20] Saint-Yves points out that "King Robert the Pious (996–1031) had an astrologer named Guido Aretinus in his service." Louis VII, having consulted the astronomer Guilaume L'Espagnol on the eclipse of July 11, 1154, decided to marry Constance of Castille in the same year. On the other hand, Louis VIII "proved to be less credulous and did not wish to believe the pronouncements of Bonet of Perpignan, who tried in vain to dissuade him from his travels abroad." For forty-four years, King Saint Louis IX had in his service Master Germain of Paluau, a physician and astrologer whom he requested to cast horoscopes for his three sons and four daughters. Philip the Bold, Philip the Fair, and Philip the Tall consulted astrologers as well. It is said that the wise King Charles V, who ruled from 1364 to 1380, had given an astrologer to Du Guesclin as part of his company. The accounts of Louis XI mention several astrologers: Pierre Chomet, Jacques Lhoste, Jean d'Orleans, and Jacques Cadot. During the reigns of later monarchs, astrologers were always well received at court. In addition, the title of astrologer was often added to that of physician. In fact, the title "physician-astrologer of the King" appears frequently in the list of gratuities.

But under Louis XIV, the death blow was dealt to official astrology. In creating the Academy of Sciences (1666), Colbert excluded from it the ancient doctrine of the heavenly bodies. To be sure, the nobles continued to have their futures predicted, but they did it secretly and, above all, as a form of entertainment. In her private journal, Mme. du Hausset, a chambermaid of Mme. de Pompadour, tells of an incident concerning Louis XV and astrology. Mme. de Pompadour had been to see a "sorceress" who had cast her horoscope. "Madame told the king of the curiosity she had had and he laughed about it, saying that it would have been amusing if the police had arrested her. But he added something very judicious: 'In order to judge the truth or falsity of such predictions,' said he, 'it would be necessary to gather together fifty of them. One would see that they almost always contain the same phrases, which sometimes are applicable and sometimes are not; no one talks of the former however—only of the latter.' "[21]

The regression of astrology was more or less generalized. And it seems that the imperative couplet of the skeptic, La Fontaine was listened to:

Charlatans, and all casters of horoscopes,
withdraw from the courts of the princes of Europe.[22]

Astrology did not die in the soul of the people, however. The proof is the undiminished popularity of the prophetic almanacs through several centuries. The oldest and most famous is the *Grand Kalendrier et Compost des Bergiers.* These almanacs, documents that are of interest to the historian, explained the influence of the planets on harvests, advised that bleeding be practiced only in a "good moon," and described in naïve terms the character of people according to the sign of their birth. All this was mixed in with the most orthodox prayers. Besides, there have always been richly embellished "books of hours," bearing reproductions of the twelve signs of the zodiac. In the nineteenth century, the advances of science would finally inter these publications.

But was this the end of astrology? Not in the least. Apart from "official" research, a movement was directed by a few rare individuals who had the laudable intention of scientifically proving the validity of astrology. This was a new idea. In 1895, in England, *Modern Astrology* was founded by Allan Leo (1860–1917). He published a work entitled *1,001 Nativities,* a collection of famous examples which, in the author's opinion, demonstrated the firm foundation of the horoscope. In France, Fomalhaut (alias Abbey

Nicoulaud) published his *Traité d'Astrologie sphérique et judiciare* (1897), a work based on mathematical assumptions, rejoining the tradition of Ptolemy. In 1902, Commander Paul Choisnard (1867–1930), a graduate of the prestigious École Polytechnique, presented the public with his *Language astral,* the first title in a long list of publications in which the author attempted to demonstrate the reality of astrology with the method of probability calculation. This meritorious effort was to leave its mark on a generation of researchers. We shall return to it later.

Parallel to this "polytechnical" astrology—and in fact unrelated to it—there was a great rebirth of interest in horoscopes between the two world wars. In fact, two currents have coexisted throughout the history of astrology without ever intermixing. One, the popular one, is that of the day-to-day magic of charlatans. The other is more cultivated, and is one where honest men—and even brilliant minds—have strived to understand and verify the influence of the stars.

This time, the popular movement has taken hold in the cities. And it is not just in France. Everywhere is found the renaissance of commercial astrology, and it has been promoted by the explosive development of modern mass media: newspapers, radio, television, and soon, computers. In the second part of the twentieth century, astrology occupies a position in our culture whose importance is visible to all.

Notes

1. *The Cosmic Clocks* H. Regnery, Chicago: 1974.

2. *La Mesopotamie,* Bloud et Gay, 1956.

3. B. L. Van der Waerden, *History of the Zodiac,* Archiv für Orientforschung, 216, 1953.

4. A. Sachs, *Babylonian Horoscope,* Institute of Cuneiform Studies, 6, no. 2, 49 (1952).

5. His *Astrologie grecque* was republished in 1963. Cutlure et Civilisation, Brussells.

6. The American Philosophical Society, Philadelphia, 1959.

7. *Astrology in Roman Law and Politics,* The American Philosophical Society: Philadelphia, 1954, pp. 59–62.

8. Cramer, *op. cit.,* in a chapter entitled "The astrologers—the power behind the throne from Augustus to Domitian."

9. L. MacNiece, *Astrology,* Aldus, 1964, p. 130.

10. Bouché-Leclercq, *op. cit.*

11. Book VII, Chapter 6. Cited by Couderc in *L'Astrologie,* Presses Universitaires de France.

12. Cited by Berthelot, *L'Astrobiologie,* Payot.

13. L. MacNiece, *Astrology.*

14. Peukert, *L'Astrologie,* Payot.

15. Op. Cit.

16. P. Couderc, *op. cit.*

17. *Encylopédie Larousse,* Vol. III, 1936.

18. *Op. cit.*

19. Lucas Dubreton, *La Renaissance italienne,* Production de Paris.

20. *Op. cit.*

21. *Le Roman de l'histoire,* Horizon de France.

22. Fable 23, Book II.

CHAPTER 3
The anatomy of the horoscope

We shall now review all the elements that permit an astrologer to elaborate and then interpret a horoscope. As a whole, it constitutes what is called *The Chart of the Heavens* at the moment of birth. It is principally composed of: twelve signs of the zodiac, ten planets, twelve "houses," and five principal "aspects."

Let us first of all establish the astronomical decor. The astrological universe is limited to our own solar system: the sun, the moon, and the planets. Its world is that of appearances. By this we mean that the heavens are envisaged as if the earth were the center of everything, and that the movements of the heavenly bodies are observed as they appear and not in accordance with their location from a cosmic perspective.

The planets

For the astrologers, there are ten heavenly bodies in the solar system. First of all there are the sun and the moon, and then, in the order of their distance from the sun: Mercury, Venus, Mars, Jupiter, Saturn, Uranus, Neptune, and Pluto.

The sun is the lord of our system, for without it, no life would exist on earth. It creates day, night, and the seasons. The gravitational force that it exerts on the earth and the other planets prevents them from being lost into the frozen infinity of space. The moon is the companion of night. Its light, a pale reflection of the sun, invites melancholia. It is a tributary of the earth, as the latter depends on the sun. But it is not without influence on us: with the aid of the sun, it brings about the phenomenon of tides.

Mercury is a small planet, representing only 5 percent of the earth's volume. It is difficult to observe, for it is often lost in the flaming rays of the sun, from which it is never far away.

Venus is about the same size as the earth. A magnificent sight that shines with a striking whiteness, it, too, is always close to the sun, but it has more freedom of action. It is the "morning star" when it precedes the sun at daybreak. It is the "evening star" when it follows the sun, brilliantly dominating the constellations in the spreading evening. Mercury and Venus are called the inferior planets, for they are the heavenly bodies that revolve between the sun and the earth.

The other planets are called superior, for their orbit is greater than that of the earth. Mars is the closest to us. It is not a large planet (one-ninth the mass of the earth), but is very intriguing, for certain of its physical conditions are rather similar to those on earth. Its reddish color has rightly struck observers from all periods of history. Farther from us majestically whirls Jupiter, the giant planet of our system. Its mass is about three hundred times that of earth. Like Venus, Jupiter shines a bright blue-white. Beyond Jupiter is Saturn which, on the contrary, has a rather weak, and flickering light, livid, gray and greenish. This negatively impressed the first observers of the heavens.

Saturn is the last of the seven planets visible to the naked eye, those traditionally used in astrology. But the English astronomer Herschel discovered Uranus in 1781. Thanks to Herschel's observations, Adams and Leverrier were able, in 1846, to calculate the place in the sky of an even more distant planet, Neptune. And finally, in 1930, the Lowell Observatory added Pluto to the list, a tiny celestial object orbiting at the limits of the solar system. Modern astrologers have annexed these three planets very quickly, and invented a language that the ancients could not have envisaged.

The zodiac

Since the days of the Chaldeans, it was known that the sun, moon, and planets followed similar paths: the zodiac. It is a zone of the celestial sphere that extends from 8.5 degrees on either side of the ecliptic, the path of the sun. As a primitive calendar, the zodiacal belt was arbitrarily divided into twelve sections of 30 degrees each. These are the famous signs of the zodiac. The origins of the names given to each sign extend into the most remote regions of antiquity. Terrestrial animal-gods, whether real or imagined, were one day projected onto the constellations which, in the Chaldean imagination, they resembled. This celestial menagerie has furthermore given the zodiac its name, for in Greek, it means "route of animals."

The sun enters the first zodiacal sign—Aries—on March 21, the spring equinox. It enters Taurus, the second sign, one month later on April 21. Thus in one year, it passes through the twelve signs of the zodiac: Aries, Taurus, Gemini, Cancer, Leo, Virgo, Libra, Scorpio, Sagittarius, Capricorn, Aquarius, and Pisces.

The moon and the planets also pass through the twelve signs, but obviously at speeds different from those of the sun. Their movement obeys Kepler's Laws. Thus the moon, which is close to the earth, circles the zodiac in twenty-nine days, while the inaccessible Pluto needs two hundred fifty years. It also happens that the planets "dawdle" along the zodiacal belt: they can be seen to slow down, stop, and even reverse directions in relationship to the constellations that they cross. These retrogradations are apparent. In reality, the planet inexorably continues along its way. But the speed of the earth itself interacts with that of the planet to occasionally give this impression.

The symbolism of the twelve signs

The very ancient tradition passed along from Manilius and Ptolemy of Alexandria ascribes well-defined properties to each sign, influences transmitted to the child at birth that determine his character, health, and destiny. Passing through the twelve signs, the planets, like so many actors, play different parts. Being born at the moment when one of the signs is occupied by several planets confers the properties of this sign on the individual. The most important presence is that of the sun, and to such an extent that one no longer says, "I was born with the sun in the sign of Scorpio," but "I am a Scorpio." It is a kind of astro-psychological calling card. And the implicit statement is: "I was born between October 23 and November 21. Be careful of me. I am critical, often mistrusting, and sometimes wicked. Moreover, it is possible for me to be drawn more than I should towards sensual pleasures," and so on.

In this way an ancient tradition has divided human beings into twelve psychological types whose descriptions are full of shrewdness and even of intuition on the profundities of human nature.

Aries, Taurus, Gemini—we have met them all in our day-to-day lives. These notations formed a kind of essay in characterological science, at a time when this science did not exist.

The interpretation of the twelve "types" that we present here constitutes a synthesis of several astrological works that in general tend to agree on the signification of the signs of the zodiac:

Aries (March 21–April 20)

Ruled by Mars, the Aries is the incarnation of violent will, impatience, impulsiveness, and rapid, often precipitated, decisions. The principal qualities are enthusiasm, courage, independence, and pride. But Aries is too aggressive and impulsive. Like the animal that symbolizes the sign, he has too great a tendency to thrust ahead with his horns without having reflected beforehand. To succeed in life the Aries must keep his enthusiasm but moderate his ardor.

Taurus (April 21–May 22)

Birth takes place in the domain of Venus, who governs this sign. In general, Taurus is a concrete being, firmly attached to the goods of this world. He has a strong but peaceful sensuality. His anger is rare, in the image of the peaceful beast that is his totem, but it comes abruptly and violently: he easily "sees red." Most often however, he demonstrates his good sense, stability and fidelity. He can sometimes be reproached for a lack of detachment and disinterestedness.

Gemini (May 21–June 21)

It is Mercury who influences the Gemini, the crafty Mercury, god of eloquence, merchants and thieves. He is above all a shrewd being, constantly proving his adaptability in all circumstances. He enjoys social contacts. All recognize Gemini's brilliance and spirituality. He must nonetheless guard against falling into easiness that would make of him a superficial, unstable and mixed-up individual. He should put intelligence in the service of a durable cause. In love, he must be careful of artificiality, and put more sincerity into rushes of feeling.

Cancer (June 22–July 22)

Like the moon that governs this sign, Cancer is an imaginative, sensitive, and dreamy individual. Somewhat self-effacing, he enjoys family life, where his timidity—and on occasion, weakness—seem to be protected from the hardness of the world. The feeling for the past is more attractive than the future. He often feels a nostalgia for childhood and the protection of his mother and must try to overcome this attitude. Cancer must strive to impose his qualities of shrewdness and intuition on groups of people. In love, it is not good for the Cancer to give too much importance to the wounds of self-love, and he must learn to declare himself at the right moment.

Leo (July 23–August 22)

Having elected to reside in this sign, the sun confers its force, amplitude, and radiance on those born in Leo. Leo is a proud, individualistic, and generous being. Authority and willpower are among the dominant character traits. Thus he has strong trump cards to help obtain success in life. Leo must be wary, however, of pride and unmeasured action, and govern ambitions with the measure of his abilities. He must avoid being too susceptible to flattery. In love, he has a tendency to transform his life into the stage of a theater. He should be more reserved in the manifestations of his rushes of feeling. Those who love him will be grateful for this.

Virgo (August 23–September 23)

It is Mercury that governs this sign. But it is not the supple and airy Mercury of Gemini. Intelligence is more matter-of-fact: less gifted but deeper. The Virgo is rightly considered to be calculating, prudent and attached to minor details to the point of fixation. For Virgo, reason overcomes the heart; precision seems to be more important than intuition, of which he is wary. In love, Virgo is not very demonstrative, or at least, being unable to decide, a late marriage will be his lot.

Libra (September 23–October 22)

Governed by Venus, the planet of harmony and the arts, one word characterizes Libra: equilibrium, as the sign symbolizes. Libra is sociable, refined, and understanding, party to conciliatory solutions. But be careful, for he is gifted with a very fine sense of justice, and will engage in battle if he considers that he has been ridiculed. In sentimental relationships, Libra is praised for his sweetness and elegance, with an occasionally somewhat exaggerated coquettishness. Aggressiveness must be stimulated, for Libra's distinguished nonchalance can prevent his social success.

Scorpio (October 23–November 21)

Mars, the god of war, and Pluto, the god of the underworld, share this kingdom. It suffices to say that the child of Scorpio is not a being of rest. There is in him a depth of violent aggressiveness and undiscipline, but also of anguish. Scorpio's enemies must contend with his piercing critical sense, which permits the rapid discovery of the chinks in their armour, for it is certain that he has flair. There is also scientific curiosity, which penetrates the depths of nature's secrets, even if they are dangerous. Passionate and jealous in love, possessing a strong sexuality; in a word, Scorpio has the best and the worst. By developing the best, he is able to have exceptional success in life.

Sagittarius (November 22–December 20)

Jupiter is the master of this sign. He confers an honest, generous, and loyal nature. Sagittarius has true nobility of character that works through goodness and moderation. He enjoys escaping from the banality of day-to-day life, and travelling attracts him. Furthermore, these travels can be imaginary as well as real. Sagittarius is a sign of the philosophic mind. In love, he prefers legality and lasting feelings to brief and violent passions and adventures.

Capricorn (December 21–January 19)

This region of the winter sky has been attributed by astrologers to the morose Saturn. Capricorn is serious, often on the defensive; decisions are taken in calm atmosphere, and he is farsighted. He is very ambitious, but is careful not to show it, preferring to act in the shadows rather than in broad daylight. It is not worth the trouble to attempt flattery, for Capricorn will not be susceptible. He is cold, objective, and wary by nature. He will not try to please in love, and some might reproach a lack of spirit; feelings exist, but they are buried deep inside. Capricorn will never sacrifice his career to a passing fling or even to a passion.

Aquarius (January 20–February 18)

Modern astrologers have assigned this sign to the planet Uranus. Like it, Aquarius is gifted with a lively intelligence, and taken by the new, sometimes by the utopian. Originality and idealism are two principal character traits. Very disinterested, Aquarius is enthused by great revolutionary causes, but will not descend into the arena. The battle of ideas is sufficient, for Aquarius always has a depth of reserve, dreaminess, and sensitivity. He is not very realistic in love, and demonstrates much independence and fantasy. He is able to please and to be devoted but does not like to become attached. Aquarius must beware of solitude.

Pisces (February 19–March 20)

Naturally it is Neptune, the god of the sea, who governs this sign. Everyone agrees that Pisces is emotive and impressionable. He is praised for intuition, poetic ability, sense of compassion, and devotion. But Pisces must overcome the indecision in his character as well as his nonchalance; for activity can suffer from them, andPisces can be thrown into a dreamy existence, one that is more than a little inefficient. Feelings are marked with a blend of mysticism and sensuality, and the feeling of sacrifice dominates.

The zodiac-man

The signs of the zodiac are certainly not assumed to influence only the character of individuals. They are also considered to play a preponderant role in health and destiny. The medieval doctrine of the zodiac-man, which has produced such a rich iconography throughout the centuries, is still used in modern medical astrology. Theoretically, each sign governs a part of the human body. Aries is assigned to the head, Taurus to the neck, and Gemini to the chest. Cancer governs the stomach, Leo the heart, Virgo the intestines, Libra the kidneys, Scorpio the sexual organs, Sagittarius the thighs, Capricorn the knees, Aquarius the calves, and Pisces the feet.

The harmony between the signs

The signs are more or less joined to one another. Depending on the harmony or opposition of their qualities, it is the same for people born in each sign. This is an important part of the horoscope, one that greatly interests the clientele: With what sign do I get along best? How should I select my friends and associates? And especially, How do I determine a marriage that conforms to the best astral formula? Several works have been published that compare the way the different signs get along with each other. The zodiacal symbolism is the key to this and plays the major determining role. Without extensive elaboration, let us consider an example, and for more details, refer the reader to specialized works.

Leo and the other signs: "A Leo and an Aries join their dynamism in the afffirmation of a will that the latter imposes, and the former slips in. Leo and Taurus find that they are more often in conflict than in complement: one wishes too much domination, and the other too much possession. Leo and Gemini quickly get along in a moment of action, and form in their collaboration a union of force and mind, of will and intelligence. Leo and Cancer are as different as day and night: as much as one is speculative, demonstrative, and imposing, the other is intimate and interior. Leo and Virgo are separated by their respective feelings of greatness and inferiority," and so forth.[1]

The symbolism of the planets

At the present time, the general public is less familiar with the symbolism of the planets than with the signs of the zodiac, although the former is probably much older. The Chaldeans, in fact, identified and deified the planets before establishing the paths they took across the heavens. A tradition that was very strong in the Middle Ages and the Renaissance created a "psychological" language of the planets that has been maintained to the present day in the majority of Latin and Anglo-Saxon languages. A "martial" gait, a "jovial" laugh, and a "lunatic" are qualifications that are directly inspired by the influence attributed by the astrologers to Mars, Jupiter, and the moon. Let us not forget either that each of the seven days in our week is dependent on a planet.[2]

Here are the principle influences that the planets are supposed to have on each of us, especially if they are in a strong position in the horoscope (taken from several modern works on astrology):

The sun

A hot and dry masculine planet. *Character:* dominated by force, vitality, ambition, and the desire for power, as well as generosity and pride. There is never lowness, but sometimes unmeasured conduct. *Health:* the sun controls the heart and the circulatory system. *Destiny:* influences young adulthood (from twenty to thirty years), predisposition to high posts and visible careers, in a word, to all the leading professions where one can be brilliant. Its day is Sunday, its metal is gold, its precious stone is the diamond, and its color is yellow.

The moon

A cold, damp feminine planet. *Character:* confers a great imagination, an ability to get along, intuition, and a feeling for poetry. Wary of inconstancy, laziness, and of the lack of strength of character. *Health:*

controls the stomach and digestion, menstruation, and lactation. *Destiny:* related to infancy. Favors employment related to education, imagination, or everything that is liquid (sailors, beverage merchants, and so on). Its day is Monday, its metal is silver, its precious stone is the natural pearl, and its color is white.

Mercury

A neutral planet that has a tendency towards the nearest heavenly body. *Character:* intelligence, vivacity of mind; astute, opportunistic, capable, having the gift of easy speech. But there is also instability, lack of depth, and wile. *Health:* controls the nervous and respiratory systems. *Destiny:* governs adolescence and favors all intellectual professions, but also journalists, orators, barkers, merchants, and . . . thieves. Its day is Wednesday, its metal is mercury, its precious stone is the opal, and its color is gray.

Venus

A hot and damp feminine planet, said to be beneficial. *Character:* love in all its forms dominates; love of life, love of fellow men, but especially just love and sexuality. A very developed sensitivity (with artistic sense) is exerted in daily life. *Health:* controls the genital-urinary system, but also the throat and the voice. *Destiny:* early childhood is under its dependence. Favors everything that touches luxury, pleasure, and art (music, painting, dance and so on). Its day is Friday, its metal is copper, its precious stone is the emerald, and its color is green.

Mars

A hot, dry masculine planet, said to be malefic. *Character:* energy, combativeness, courage, and decisiveness. But in addition to this, there is impulsiveness, violence, and a too-pronounced taste for struggle. *Health:* governs the muscular system, but also the arteries. *Destiny:* favors the forties, as well as all activities that call for a certain risk and much action (military careers, surgery, and exploration). Its day is Tuesday, its metal is iron, its precious stone is the ruby, and its color is red.

Jupiter

A hot and damp masculine planet, said to be beneficent. *Character:* desire to profit from life in all its forms but in general, within strictly "middle-class" norms. Loves money and "high living," but is also a defender of justice and the established order. *Health:* governs the liver and the blood. *Destiny:* favors financial success towards sixty years of age for all who enter business, adminstration, law, and banking. Its day is Thursday, its metal is tin, its precious stone is the sapphire, and its color is blue.

Saturn

A cold, dry masculine planet, said to be malefic. *Character:* confers qualities of seriousness, reserve, and depth, but can lead to selfishness, bitterness, and pessimism. *Health:* controls the bones and skin. *Destiny:* influences old age, and leads to activities in relationship with the earth and minerals (farmers, miners, and speleologists). Also favors life in laboratories and in libraries. Its day is Saturday, its metal is lead, its precious stone is jade, and its color is black.

Uranus

Sometimes said to be the "electromagnetic" planet. *Character:* originality, independence, passion, and self-affirmation can often be turned into systematization, eccentricity, utopianism, and even megalomania. *Health:* controls the nervous system. *Destiny:* promises success to all those who enter careers in technology. Protects inventors, electricians, and . . . astrologers. Found in dictators. A new planet, Uranus has no day, but it is attributed uranium as its metal, amethyst as its precious stone, and violet as its color.

Neptune

In general, said to be feminine and damp. *Character:* predisposed to mysticism, chimeras, and inconsistency, but also the quality of intuition, even paranormal gifts. *Health:* danger from epidemics, as well as the possibility of psychic problems. *Destiny:* favors crowds, demagoguery, and anarchy. But in addition, it exerts a fortunate influence on poets and mystics. Its attributes have not yet been established.

Pluto

Astrologers have only had forty years to determine its influence. On the whole, they find it to be malefic governing the demonic side of life, immanent justice, and great upheavals. It is used widely in "world" astrology. The naming of the planet after the god of the underworld is in fact not very appealing. In spite of this however, astrologers will no doubt remember as a comfort that the symbol used to represent Pluto (a *P* and an *L* intertwined) finds its origin not only in the first two letters of the planet's name, but also in the initials of the astronomer Percival Lowell, whose calculations permitted its discovery.

The twelve houses

The doctrine of astrological houses is a typically Greek invention. It is found romantically described in Manilius' *Astronomicon,* the vast astrological poem dating to the beginnings of our era that we have mentioned above. The doctrine of "houses" has passed unchanged through twenty centuries of history, and it is found in the complete horoscope cast by the modern astrologer. When spoken to of houses, the neophyte is generally a little lost. In fact, their comprehension demands a higher degree of astrological initiation than that required for the understanding of the zodiac and the planets. Their definition is not self-evident; for this reason, the delimiting of houses in the heavens has always been a source of debate among astrologers. These debates have not ceased in the twentieth century. There are several systems of domification (from the Latin *domus* = house), each of which having its adherents. The principle ones are those of Placidus, Regiomontanus, and Campanus, not to mention the more modern inventions. We shall not however, enter into these technical controversies here.

The astronomical definition

The exact moment of birth must be known in order to calculate the houses. While the position of the planet in the signs of the zodiac depends on the day, month, and year, its position in the houses depends essentially on the place and the hour. The houses are established according to the rotation of the earth on its axis in twenty-four hours (its *diurnal movement*). Like the sun, all the heavenly bodies appear to move around the celestial sphere in one day, as a result of this movement. Struck by the alternation of day and night, astrologers began to consider the day to be a small model of a year. And in the same way that they divided the zodiac into twelve signs, they divided the diurnal movement into twelve houses. Thus, for a given place and moment, the celestial sphere is divided like an orange into twelve slices. The boundaries of the houses are fixed on the ecliptic, the center of the route of the planets. These boundaries are called *cusps* of the houses. Each planet passes through the twelve houses in twenty-four hours. This is why for the astrologer, the exact hour of birth is essential.

The ascendant

The houses are numbered from one to twelve beginning with the ascendant, and in the reverse of diurnal movement (traditionally, Roman numerals are used to number them). The ascendant is thus a very important element in the horoscope. It is the point of the zodiac that rises in the East at the moment of birth. All astrologers agree that the rising sign is at least as important as the birth sign. The Greek astrologers, the inventors of the ascendant, called it simply *horoscope*. The fact that this word has come to designate the whole of the birth chart indicates the esteem in which this astrological factor has been held down through the centuries. In spite of this however, the ascendant was only known to specialists until the popular publications transmitted the notion to their readers, in order to put some diversity in their daily predictions. "Perhaps you do not have the sign you think." In fact, the solar sign and the rising sign have an equal importance for the astrologer. Their influences are wedded.[3]

The intensity of the houses

The twelve astrological houses are divided into three levels of intensity. The maximal power goes to the four houses that precede the horizon and the meridian (in astrology, the *angles* of the horoscope); they are houses I, IV, VII, and X. They are called the *cardinal houses.*

The next four houses (and thus their name of *succeeding houses*) have a medium intensity. They are houses II, V, VIII, and XI.

The last four houses have a weak, sometimes even evil influence, and thus their pejorative name of *cadent houses.* They are houses III, VI, IX, and XII.

The house confers its strength or weakness on the planet located in it. Thus Mars in the first house will be strong in the horoscope; in the second house, it will be less so; and in the twelfth house, its intensity will be minimum.

The symbolism of houses

The houses are said to be the portions of the heavens that govern different sectors of human life. Here are their principle attributes:

House I: characteristic aptitudes and physical appearance of the subject.

House II: financial gains; everything the subject earns by himself.

House III: brothers and sisters, but also writings and short journeys.

House IV: father and mother, but also family, home, and later life.

House V: pleasures, loves, distractions, and, by implication, children.

House VI: work, but also employees and small animals; in addition, painful illnesses.

House VII: marriage, and, by implication, associates, and . . . declared enemies.

House VIII: death and inheritances.

House IX: long journeys and large animals; in addition, religion and philosophy.

House X: profession, success, and honors.

House XI: friends, relations, and advisors.

House XII: trials, chronic illnesses, prisons, and hospitals: all sorts of misfortunes.

Planetary aspects

The planets seem to move through the zodiacal signs at different speeds. Day by day then, these movements cause them to meet or to be separated from one another, while there is formed between them apparent angular relationships that the terrestrial observer can measure. Out of the possible angles between 0 degrees and 180 degrees, astrologers have for a very long time been interested in certain angles considered to be crucial points, for they describe geometrical figures along the zodiacal belt: these are the astrological "aspects" formed by the planets at the moment of birth. There are five principle aspects: conjunction, sextile, quarter, trine, and opposition.

Conjunction: two planets that are found at the same degree of the zodiac or very close to one another. It is a very important aspect and its meaning depends on the planets in question. The conjunctions of Mars and Saturn are bad, while those of Venus and Jupiter are good.

The sextile: two planets separated from one another by 60 degrees. This is an aspect where the two planets harmoniously blend their influences. It is less powerful than the trine, however.

The square: two planets separated by 90 degrees. It is an evil and violent aspect, one where the planetary influxes collide. About the square, astrologers point out that when moon and the sun are squared, their gravitational effects are partly eliminated, producing the weakest tides.

The trine: two planets separated by 120 degrees. This is the best possible aspect: powerful and beneficial at the same time. A horoscope with many trines is a measure of a happy life.

Opposition: two planets separated by 180 degrees. Astrologers consider this to be a bad aspect, for the influence of the two planets are in opposition, they are situated at opposite extremes of the firmament. They do not point out however, that when the moon and the sun are in opposition, their gravitational effects, far from eliminating one another, combine to produce strong tides.

The orb of aspects: absolutely exact aspects are rare. It is infrequent, for example, that Mars be exactly 90 degrees from Saturn (which would be called a *partile* square). The principle of allowing a certain latitude in the exactitude of the aspect is not questioned by astrologers: it is called the *orb* of the aspect, the point beyond which it ceases to be effective. On the other hand however, there is a lively discussion as to how large a latitude may be allowed. Some permit a variation of 10 degrees to either side of the precise aspect, and others only 5 degrees. The most rigorous seek an exactitude within one degree.

Interpretation

At the moment of a child's birth, the clockwork system of the celestial roulette wheel seems to stop for a moment—for the child, at least—in a horoscope. The chart of the heavens is sometimes compared to a photographic slide, where the astrologer is the photographer and the child is the film. The planets are dispersed in various ways in the signs of the zodiac and the houses, and they generate a certain number of aspects, and so on. All this constitutes the texture of the child's destiny and character. But for the astrologer, the most important and most delicate task remains to be accomplished: the development of the film, the interpretation of the chart of the heavens.

The indications that we have presented above form the basis of every consultation, but they are only fixed definitions, only little units of destinies. The horoscope is a structural organic whole where each astrological factor plays its harmonious or dissonant melody in the symphony of multiple influences that are in play. Let us take an example: a child is born with the sun in the nonchalant and dreamy sign of Cancer; but his ascendant is in Scorpio, the sign of the aggressive and warlike Mars. The astrologer must consider that these two tendencies exist conjointly in the child. For the interpretation of this effect, almost all the manuals of astrology contain much more detailed categories than those we have presented. In particular, there are always two chapters of very useful formulae entitled: "The Planets in the Signs," and "The Planets in the Houses." In fact, it has classically been admitted that the symbolism of its planets is wedded to that of their celestial location.

Here is what an astrologer predicts about an individual with Venus in Leo: "high or imperious amorous aspirations, with passions that are free and full, total and radiant." But if a child is born a few days later, when Venus has left Leo and entered Virgo, its amorous disposition will be radically changed. The verdict of the same astrologer is: "Feelings are reserved, discrete, timid, and prudish, drawn towards purity or a state of inferiority." One can see the restrictions borne by the timorous influence of the sign of Virgo.

But Venus is also found in a house. And that gives an indication of the type of activity that will be affected by the planet. "The sector where Venus is located," says the astrologer, "is a place where the subject enjoys love, affection, sympathy, or the favor of others." Is Venus in the seventh house? "The planet of love in the marriage sector is one of the best possible positions." But what if the child is born two hours later, when Venus is in the eighth house? Nothing works anymore: "It causes the fear of loss of loved ones and may correspond to widowhood."

And finally, Venus receives a certain number of aspects from the other planets, and this provides the beneficial or evil tonality of the prediction. Let Venus find itself in conjunction with Saturn, and it is the end of amorous flights, portending misfortune for all feelings. On the other hand, Venus trine Jupiter is a measure of joy and harmony.

The reader will understand the difficulty in interpreting the horoscope. Everything affects everything, and the synthesis is incessantly put in question. When an astrologer says "This person has Venus in Virgo conjunction Saturn in the seventh house," it means that this person will probably remain single and it is no doubt all for the better. But if the whole of the horoscope is good, if Jupiter is in the fifth house, that of love, and is surrounded with background of good aspects, the unfortunate prediction can be at least partly revised.

The date of events

The natal horoscope gives precise indications about the physical and mental dispositions of the child, as it does for the factors that condition his destiny. But human nature is not content with vague predictions; its restless curiosity needs more substantial nourishment. This is why astrologers have always strived to satisfy their clients by indicating precise dates for the principal events of their lives. The ancient Greeks excelled in this art. These methods are all based on a fundamental principle: the horoscope at birth does not abruptly stop influencing the child once the moment of birth has passed. It contains the virtuality of the child's future. It can be structured in time. Thus one can precisely predict the dates that the natal horoscope only indicates.

The present work is not an astrological treatise, and we will content ourselves with defining three of the principal methods used by modern astrologers to provide the dates for the events of someone's life: *transits, directions,* and *solar revolutions.*

Transits

These are the passages of the planets through particularly "sensitive" points of the birth horoscope. In passing through these crucial regions in an individual's zodiac—or, if you prefer, in transiting them—the passing planet exerts a phenomenon of activation that can provoke a good or bad event. Here is an example given by an astrologer: General Charles DeGaulle's ascendant is at 21 degrees of Libra. Now, if one consults the *emphemeris* for the month of May 1958, the moment of his return to power, it is seen that the *beneficial* Jupiter was at this same degree of the zodiac. It thus transited the ascendant of the general. This could only, it seems to the astrologer, favor the plans of the future president of France.

Directions

There are several kinds: primary, secondary, symbolic, and so on. All are based on analogy and use the fictive passing of the planets through the circle of birth. They allow predictions to be made to the year. Let us take the example of symbolic directions. The procedure consists in fictively displacing the planets of the heavens at birth, with one degree of the zodiac corresponding to one year in the life of the individual. Here is an example of the surprising efficacity of this system, given by an astrologer and applied to the horoscope of General DeGaulle. The general's sun is at 29 degrees 50' of Scorpio, and Jupiter at 6 degrees 53' of Libra; 67 degrees separate these two planets. Since according to the symbolic postulate of the system one degree equals one year, it can be noted that the sun rejoins the beneficial Jupiter in the general's sixty-seventh year: that is, his age upon his return to power.

Solar revolutions

The importance of the sun's position in a horoscope makes it possible to use it to evaluate the tonality of a given year in the life of an individual. A solar revolution is a "classical" horoscope calculated for the moment of the "astrological birthday" of the subject, that is, for the moment when the sun passes precisely over the position it occupied at birth. For DeGaulle, the solar revolution—or his yearly horoscope—is calculated for the passage of the sun into 29 degrees 50' of Scorpio. The birthday horoscope can be good or bad in itself, but predictions for the year to come can only be made by establishing careful comparisons with the natal horoscope, which is always the frame of reference. Modern astrologers and their clientele attach great importance to "solar revolutions." This is because they consider it to be a way of combatting misfortune: they can spend their birthday far from their homes. In fact, the exact hour when the sun passes over the natal position varies according to where one is on the globe. If one calculates in advance that the malefic Saturn will be in one's ascendant in New York at a certain moment, the blow can be avoided. It suffices to take a trip at that moment, a voyage to Europe, for example. This would noticeably separate Saturn from the ascendant and save the individual from the health problems to which he would have inevitably been exposed if he had not taken a trip. These astrologically inspired vacations demand financial means. And this is the solution adopted ten years ago—on the advice of his astrologer—by the head of a large company who confidentially related the story to us.

A sample interpretation

Every astrological treatise ends with a sample interpretation, usually the horoscope of a famous person. And we shall not be lacking in this respect. We shall choose that of General DeGaulle. It has been noted however, that those interested enough in astrology to cast a complete chart of the heavens always begin with their own. Thus we would have liked to allow each reader the possibility of proceeding in this manner. But to establish one's own chart, one must acquire the voluminous ephemeris that indicate the daily positions of the

planets, as well as a table of houses. We must be content with show-
ing how the whole of an astrological theme is interpreted.

General DeGaulle was born in the city of Lille in the north of
France on November 22, 1890, at 4:00 in the morning, according to
official records. Astronomical calculations for this date give the
chart of the heavens shown in Chart 3.1.

By using only the astrological assumptions in Chart 3.1, we can
evaluate the character, health, and destiny of General DeGaulle.
Let us limit ourselves to the essential however, referring the reader
to the numerous astrological publications that have analyzed his
horoscope for a fuller portrait. For us here it is above all a didactic
illustration of what precedes.

Chart 3.1
General DeGaulle

Sun	29° Scorpio in the House II
Moon	4° Aries in the House VI
Mercury	2° Sagittarius in the House II
Venus	18° Sagittarius in the House II
Mars	11° Aquarius in the House IV
Jupiter	7° Aquarius in the House IV
Saturn	16° Virgo in the House XI
Uranus	29° Libra in the House I
Neptune	5° Gemini in the House VIII
Pluto	7° Gemini in the House VIII
Ascendant	21° Libra

The notable aspects are:
Ascendant conjunction Uranus
Sun conjunction Mercury
Mars conjunction Jupiter
Moon sextile Neptune
Saturn square Venus
Sun trine Moon
Mercury trine Moon
Sun opposition Neptune
Mercury opposition Neptune

Character

The sun is in Scorpio and the ascendant is in Libra. Their influences are contradictory. Scorpio is the aggressive, violent and undisciplined critical mind that dissolves everything, flair, and the art of making enemies. Libra, on the contrary, confers understanding, the spirit of conciliation, sweetness, and the sense of justice. These elements must thus coexist in the general's character, creating in him what is called a "psychical polarity." Furthermore, since it is found in the first house, that of character, account must be taken of a strong Uranus in the horoscope. Uranus adds to the whole an element of independence, authority, self-affirmation, even excessiveness. Intelligence and imagination are good (Mercury in a good relationship with the moon) but passionate, for the moon is in Aries. Feelings are strong (Venus is in Sagittarius), but they are cold and sullen as a result of the negative relationship between Saturn and Venus. Finally, the opposition between Saturn and Neptune can lead to illusions and to mysticism.

Destiny

The general's horoscope has no planet in the tenth house, which is somewhat surprising. A strong Uranus promises success to technicians however, to inventors (tanks?[4]), and to all those who profit from unexpected and explosive situations (1940, 1958?[5]). The presence of the conjunction between Jupiter (success) and Mars (violence) in the fourth house (the end of life) accents the importance of this period of the subject's life.[6] The moon (popularity) is situated in a weak house (VI) however, and in a sign that does not coincide with its nature (Aries). In truth, few things in this horoscope indicate a real military vocation. It is the chart of a dynamic inventor with an agitated career, rather than that of a president of a nation—at least according to astrological symbolism.

Health

Scorpio is a sign of strong vitality, but Libra confers a less strong resistance. The presence of Uranus would predispose a nervousness, a certain lack of self-control. The moon in the sixth house (acute illnesses) in Aries (the head) must be pointed out. There are hardly any indications that can explain how the general reached the age of eighty without serious illness. Let us note the presence of the shadowy Pluto in a poor relationship in the eighth house, that of death, which increases the risk of assassination.

This—more or less—is what an astrologer has to say after examining DeGaulle's horoscope. We say "more or less" because the inextricable network of influences in play permit a great many variations, some of which are contradictory. Some have even gone so far as to radically modify the general's hour of birth, in order to put the heavens in better agreement with a desired destiny.

Let us not forget how much the attitude of the interpreter can differ, depending on whether he must predict the future of a child in its cradle, or explain a destiny as exceptional as that of General DeGaulle after the fact. The reader will have noticed how much the preceding interpretation of the general's horoscope corresponds to reality. It is because in the choice of meanings we have posited for the presage we have voluntarily played the astrologer's game. Besides, in the gamut of influences that are presented, it is almost impossible not to choose those that correspond most closely to a man's destiny when one knows that destiny. No one can escape, whether astrologer or not. This is why the scientist prefers to mistrust the astrological "art" and to judge it with the help of more objective criteria that permit unanimity on the validity of the horoscope. We shall return to this later.

Notes

1. *Leo,* Editions du Seuil.
2. In French, the days of the week are: lundi (Monday-Moon), mardi (Tuesday-Mars), mercredi (Wednesday-Mercury), jeudi (Thursday-Jupiter), vendredi (Friday-Venus), and samedi (Saturday-Saturn). NT
3. It is not difficult to calculate the rising sign; it demands astronomical tables that are too voluminous to reproduce here. We would therefore refer the reader to the many specialized works.
4. DeGaulle wrote three books on mechanized warfare in the 1930s. NT
5. In 1940, DeGaulle established the French Government in London after the Nazi victory. In 1958, he assumed control of the government in the midst of the Algerian crisis. NT
6. Like Churchill, many of DeGaulle's political accomplishments occured after the age of 65. NT

CHAPTER 4
Astrological dogma

Once the horoscope is known, a question comes to mind: What is the nature of the planetary influences and how is the narrow connection between man's destiny and the paths of the planets explained?

In *L'Astrologie grecque*, Bouché-Leclercq writes:

> Astrology's principal dogmas are based on the following propositions:
>
> By virtue of universal solidarity or sympathy, the planets exert on the earth—and especially on man, who has affinities with the whole world—an action that is in harmony with their nature and in proportion with their power.
>
> This action is exerted by currents of force or rectilinear effluvia and tends to assimilate the object, the person who receives action, to the agent of this action, the point of arrival to the point of departure.
>
> It depends on the position of the planets . . . [and] is exerted at the moment of birth with such an intensity that it irrevocably fixes destiny, which is henceforth independent or almost independent of ulterior opportunities.

Bouché-Lerclercq's text implicitly contains the two great theories defended and used by astrologers to explain the influence of heavenly bodies such as they conceive it. The first is that of universal sympathy or solidarity; it is called the *symbolist theory.* The second is that of currents of force and effluvia; it is called the *physical theory.*

The Greeks were the first to question the origin of astral influences. At the time of the rudimentary astrology of the Chaldeans, these influences were self-evident. The priest-astrologers experienced "no difficulty in conceiving how and why the gods acted: they acted because it pleased them and they wanted to," says Bouché-Leclercq. Faced with stronger and stronger criticism, later centuries saw astrologers obliged to propose more and more extended explanations of astral influence, and this more than ever in our own century.

Universal sympathy

The Emerald Table, an old hermetic text, states:

It is true and not false, certain and veritable
That what is high is like what is low
And that what is low is like what is high
So that the miracle of unity can be perpetuated.

This voluntarily naive quatrain sums up an ancient and venerable explanation of man's place in the universe. More than an explanation, it is a religion or an astral philosophy. A tradition has been perpetuated from Pythagoras to the modern thinker, passing through Plato and Aristotle. For the astral mysticism of the Pythagoreans, the planets "imitated the circular and uniform movement of intelligence," and afterwards, the soul of the dead returned to the stars that brought them forth; in this way the universal harmony is established. For Plato, souls descended from the stars and then, once life was ended, returned to them. These conceptions were later crystallized in the famous doctrine of *macrocosm* and *microcosm:* the entire universe has mysterious sympathetic links to the miniscule interior cosmos of each individual.

The increasing complexity of Greek astrology necessitated a precise application of this doctrine of planetary influx. This was the contribution of Plotinus (205-270), a neo-Platonic philosopher of Christian tendencies. In his *Enneaes,* he gives the most complete explanation of "the influence of the planets," envisaging it as a cosmic sympathy. "The world is a single animal . . . the events here below take place in sympathy with heavenly things" (IV, 4, 34). Since all events are coordinated and converge towards unity, they are all announced in signs . . .; the planets, which are an important part of the heavens, collaborate in the universe. These magnificent beings serve as signs; they portend all that happens in the sensible world; but they are not the cause of events (II, 3, 8). The soul of the universe is the active cause, it is the breath of the great animal (IV, 3, 33). Plotinus suggests the image of a dancer: "It is to the movements of this dancer that those of the heavens must be compared. It is thus that celestial things announce events, this state of things corresponds to that situation, that position and that figure. Not that the beings forming these figures are the active causes." It will be noted that this explanation was accepted by certain Church fathers, who admired the distinction between astral signs and astral causes: for the Church, the "souls, the breath of the great animal" is God Himself. Nevertheless, Plotinus's explanation is very close to the level of horoscopic prediction, particularly when he states elsewhere: "One can say that Jupiter is blessing and Mars frightening, for it is through the former that happy events are expressed and through the latter, unhappy events."

We find a very similar conception in the work of Raymond Abellio, a contemporary French philosopher. For Abellio, whose explanations are somewhat obscure and vague, only "the symbolist astrologers take the multivalence of each aspect into account; . . . they are thus led each time to propose a more or less wide set of symbolically related significations that are nonetheless distinct, and to announce climates or tendencies more than precise events." In fact, astrology is above all a "dialectical image of the world system. [It] proposes a complete and totally enveloping structure from the outset, one that can be called a 'universal' or 'absolute' structure. Thus constituted, astrology appears as the completed structural model of all human and physical sciences, and in a way, their immanent *telos*.[1] Astrology would thus be structural! And in modern philosophical language the idea,—an idea whose perenniality down through the centuries is so worthy of attention—that astrology is not only the mother of every science, but of every philosophy, is again expressed. If it does not end up in a religion, it is at least "wisdom."

During the Renaissance, Kepler had the idea of pushing the analogy of universal harmonies even further. According to these analogies, children were supposedly born with horoscopes similar to those of their ancestors.[2] The fortune or misfortune of the parents would automatically fall upon the descendants, who inherited a comparable portion of the world's soul. This "astral heredity," in reality very close to the Hindu doctrine of the Karma, made its way into the twentieth century when Paul Choisnard tried in vain to give it statistical validity.[3] Nonetheless, many symbolist astrologers still believe in this astral heredity.

Appplication of the theory

But what happens to the horoscope in all this? Is not this astral philosophy far distant from the "basely material" point of view of those who use the planetary configurations to pierce the mystery of their destiny? On the contrary, respond many of the more important modern astrologers; this theory is the key that explains the horoscope better than any other.

The doctrine of reestablished harmonies descends daily into its arena to explain and predict the future. In reality, one only has to refer to the preceding chapter to be convinced of this. The theory of the man-zodiac posits that the macrocosm of the constellations has its analogical homologue in the human body. The malefic Saturn is in the sign of Leo at the moment of birth, and the individual is struck directly in the heart of his microcosmic organism, for Leo symbolizes the heart. Charactericial tendencies are explained in the same way: Libras are "well-balanced," criticism from Scorpios is like a poisonous bite; there is also an analogy for profession: there are more sailors who are Pisces, and mountain climbers will be in sympathy with Capricorn, whose goat *(capra)* is the symbol of dizzying ascent; jockeys will have an affinity with the sign of Saggitarius, the half-man, half-horse centaur. This analogical mimetism will of course extend to the other elements of the horoscope, to the planets and the houses. Since Mars is seen to be red, it is the planet of soldiers, killers, and others who spill blood. As for the twelfth house, situated just after the rising of the planet, it is the worst of all. Twenty centuries ago, Manilius furnished the symbolic explanation for this in his poem: "The planet that has just risen behind the horoscope [that is, the ascendant] risks sliding down the incline." (Manilius II, p. 899).

This conception is manifestly "antiscientific," in today's sense of the word. For the man of science, and the psychologist in particular, analogy is a primitive means of explaining the world, one that precedes logic and causality in the history of thought. But the symbolists do not feel threatened by such criticism. They consider that what is antiscientific today might not be tomorrow, when new progress in knowledge will cause analogy and symbolism to triumph once again. This is why they proudly reject every "physical" compromise in explaining the nature of astral influence. The astrologer who interprets birth according to external planets is mistaken; they do not affect man. "It is the interior heaven with its planets that acts," said Paracelsus in the sixteenth century. And a modern astrologer goes farther when he writes: "For this symbolist astrology, there is a knowledge of universal correspondences and no more mechanical necessity, physical action or causal relationship."

Effluvia and rays

Other astrologers resolutely dispute the validity of such assumptions. For them, astrology is neither an art nor a philosophy, and even less a religion. It is a true science. The planets are not chimeras, but are very real objects. So why would they not associate birth with *rays* that determine character and destiny? Like some "sensitive plate," the child would be "imprinted" for his whole life by the stellar influxes that are present the day of his coming into the world. In very ancient times, the great Ptolemy explained the influence of the planets with arguments borrowed from physics. For example, he grouped the planets into those that were hot or cold, dry or wet, and masculine or feminine—properties that accounted for their action. Jupiter is benefic, he states in his *Tetrabiblos,* because it is a "temperate planet situated between the fires of Mars and the ice of Saturn." A controversy between Ptolemy and another astrologer, Dorothy of Sidon, confirms this preoccupation with finding material explanations for astral influences; it was over whether the ascendant or the midheaven was more important in a horoscope: "The *physicists* found good reasons for affirming the supremacy of the meridian. The horoscope [the ascendant], they said, only sends to earth a ray that is oblique and diluted by the haze of the horizon, while the planet culminating at the meridian is at its maximum energy and causes the fire of its rays to bend straight down on the heads of men. The partisans of the supremacy of the horoscope opposed this irrefutable physical argument with one from physiology and metaphysics: that the horoscope signals growth and rising, while decline begins at the culmination. Thus the question remained always undecided, with Ptolemy arguing for the meridian, and Dorothy of Sidon sustaining the prerogative of the horoscope.[4]

The arguments of the physicists at the time were necessarily rudimentary. They knew nothing about the composition of the planets, the nature of their shining or their distances from the earth. Accounting for all the elements of a horoscope with physics was only an estimation. At most, the effect of the sun and moon on the tides had permitted the ancients to justify the doctrine of astrological aspects. When they were "squared," did not the effects of sun and moon oppose one another to give the earth the weakest marine oscillation? In consequence, it was deduced that every "squared" aspect had to be bad.

But the twentieth century has nourished the hopes of astrologers and assured the triumph of the physical theory of astrology. For fifty years or more, strange discoveries have been accumulating in physics. X-Rays, gamma and cosmic rays, and radio waves that come from the depths of the universe are an invitation to new explanations. And they are multiplying. One astrologer claims that the lines of force of the earth's magnetic field justify the division of the heavens into twelve signs or houses: another invents new rays—the Odic ray—that justify the whole horoscope. Here is a more detailed explanation: "At the moment of birth, the child undergoes this first flood of cosmic waves, which imprints its unerasable mark, indelibly inscribing the living cells like a stylus traces marks on a disc of virgin wax. It is easily understood how each of us has a wave modulated according to characteristics that are proper to him."[5]

These theoreticians have against them both scientists, who consider their pretentions an "abuse of determinism," and their symbolist colleagues, who treat scientific astrology as a "mythology of replacement." The gulf between astrophysics and the horoscope is, it is true, quite deep.

Determinism and free will

Whether material or immaterial, the influence of the planets is the cause of our destiny. Thus, since his appearance in the world, has man been unfree?

In the days of the Chaldeans, there was no appeal from the all-powerful god-lights. Free will did not exist. Commercial astrology of the twentieth century is also almost totally ignorant of this word. But down through the centuries many thinkers—and in particular those associated with Christianity—have tried to eliminate a paradox: the association of the freedom of each human being to save his soul with a rigorous astral determinism. Man can struggle against cosmic influences. "The wise man governs his star, while the fool is governed by it," states an ancient adage taken up by saint Thomas Aquinas: *"Sapiens dominabitur astris."* In fact, the slogan for the majority of astrologers is the oft-repeated motto: *"Astra inclinant, non necessitant":* the planets induce tendencies, but they do not determine.

It would not be good form for a serious practitioner today to oppose this aphorism, which is furthermore a necessary prudence towards the law and possible disgruntled clients. It can certainly not be denied that the tendencies inscribed in the horoscope follow the client all his life; but the manifestation of the prediction might occur on different levels. It is there that man's free will can intervene. If there is a portent of violent death by airplane accident in our birth sky, this cannot happen if we systematically refuse to use this means of travel or to visit airports. But this is a trivial example. Here is another one: a man's horoscope shows strong dissonances between the sun and Mars, which are situated in fourth and eighth houses respectively (parents and death). It is an indication that there will be a violent conflict between the bearer of this horoscope and his father. There is a clear desire of the man to kill his father and be rid of him, for his father appears as an obstacle in his path. It is not reasonable however, to predict to this individual that he will kill his father: the tendency will certainly exist, but perhaps it will remain unconscious. The subject might be content with killing his father in a dream, for example. In a word, the form of the prediction will be dependent on the person's level of evolution. The higher it is, the more effective is the role played by free will in channeling the malefic influxes or on the contrary, magnifying favorable aspects.

Psychological astrology

All contemporary astrologers defend one point of view: planets do not necessarily act upon exterior events, but rather they act within the individual's psyche. "Saturn exists not in the heavens, but within us," said Paracelsus. Forty years ago, Dr. Allendy revised this conception of interior destiny.[6] And today there is a veritable outbidding everywhere the horoscope is practiced. Whether or not it is in good faith, astrologers of all countries imagine that they are the inventors of this "modern" astrology. We are in the age of psychological astrology, like the sixteenth century was that of the prophecies of Nostradamus. We must cite the names of a few pioneers, however. In France, Paul Choisnard published his *Essai de psychologie astrale* in 1925; about 1935, K.E. Krafft founded a school of

Typocosmie in Switzerland. In Germany, we can mention Von Klöcker and H. A. Strauss; in England, C. O. Carter; and in the United States, Dane Rudhar.

This conception has so penetrated the mind of the public that charlatans are obliged to make sacrifices to psychology in their classified advertisements. Sometimes they declare that they are "astro-psychological counselors," sometimes that they are graduates of some "Institute of Advanced Psychological Studies"; this is done without shame or risk, because to this day the title of "graduate psychologist" is not yet protected by the law in France, as is a doctor of medicine, for example. Many recent works have sought to explain the horoscope with the new ideas of modern psychology: characterology, Jung's introverted and extroverted types, the eight characters of Le Senne, Kretschmer's three temperaments, Pavlov's conditioned reflex, and Freudian psychoanalysis, have all been pretexts for the elaboration of systematized doctrines. The marriage of astrology and psychoanalysis is no doubt a fascinating one. Many astrologers are also graphologists, and modern morphopsychology uses astrological expressions to describe the human face: "Moon type," "Mars type," and "Mercury type" are a sure aftermath to astral physiognomy of the Middle Ages.

A disturbing paradox

Reflecting on it however, it can be seen that this psychological mode is based on a misunderstanding. For today, like yesterday, astrology remains above all "the art of predicting the future," as the dictionary defined it: This is its fundamental vocation. The most psychological of astrologers nonetheless continues to predict the lucky and unlucky periods of his client's lives. For their part, the clients no doubt greatly appreciate an analysis of their character, but prefer a hundred times more to know what the future has in store for them. A certain blindness is needed in wishing to reconcile this interior astrology with the strokes of good and bad luck that Jupiter or Saturn provoke by passing through the heavens at the moment of birth.

There is no doubt that this incompatibilty between psychological and predictive astrology is today the principle stumbling block for every serious explanation of the mystery of astral influences. One can give many examples of this uneasiness.

To illustrate the idea that astrology and psychoanalysis have in fact the same object, an astrologer cites the famous apostrophe that an *aide de camp* hurls at Wallenstein in one of Schiller's plays: "It is in your heart that the stars of your destiny are found!" meaning that nothing happens to us that we do not produce ourselves. But it is the same astrologer who writes elsewhere that Napoleon's death on Saint Helena on May 5, 1821 is "easily" explained, because "the moon transited his planet—Venus at 7 degrees of Cancer—which was situated in sector eight; and this moon in a way transferred on Venus the opposition that—at the third degree of Capricorn— Uranus and Neptune dispatched to this planet situated in the seventh house"(!!)[7] There is no question here of interior destiny. No psychology can explain such conclusions, and free will is replaced by the most blind determinism.

And what can be said about the ever larger number of astrologers that calculate the dates of worldwide crises, wars and catastrophes by following the course of the planets in the ephemeris? Less in world astrology than in individual astrology do these practices seem in agreement with the idea of a horoscope that would only furnish the characteristic tendencies of personality. It seems then, that it is by denying their own theory that the astro-psychologers announce future events.

The explanation of C. G. Jung

The well-known Swiss psychologist and psychoanalyst Carl Gustav Jung (1876-1961) attempted to give a solution to this dilemma, a solution that seemed to him able to reconcile the symbolist and physical interpretations of astrology. Jung wanted to be a universal mind and was curious about almost everything. If his most important contribution is in the field of psychology and his development of the theory of the collective unconscious and archetypes, Jung also investigated subjects as different and controversial as alchemy, flying saucers, and Picasso. Thus it is not surprising that, interested in everything that touched human psychology, he came to be interested in astrology.

One thing is certain: Jung did not profess the disdain of the majority of contemporary scholars in regards to the possible influence of the planets. And from the outset, one might consider him to be more than sympathetic when he writes: "If some authors of mediocre education have believed until now that they could ridicule astrology as having vanished long ago, this same astrology, rising in the soul of the people, presents itself once again today at the gates of the university that it left three hundred years ago."[8]

To this favorable declaration about astrology can be added the responses Jung made in an interview in 1954: "There have been many cases of striking analogy between the horoscope and characterological disposition. There is even the possibility of a certain prediction."[9] Later, he notes that during psychoanalytical treatment, he had observed a distinct influence of astral passages, "particularly the affections of Saturn and Uranus." According to him these planets might be the cause of problems in psychoanalysis.

Jung's opinion seems clear and somewhat surprising. Nevertheless, he remarks still later that "the horoscope seems to correspond to a certain moment of the mutual maintenance of the gods, which means of psychic archetypes." This is already more ambiguous. Did the great psychoanalyst believe in a "special" astrology? In fact, Jung constructed a whole theory of the mind around the astrological idea. It has often been poorly understood. We shall attempt to give a brief exposition of it.

It all seems to have begun with a rather astonishing adventure Jung had and that he relates in a book he wrote in collaboration with W. Pauli, a Nobel Prize winner in physics: *Naturerklarung und Psyche* (The Interpretation of Nature and the Psyche).[10] Jung decided one day to test by experiment one of the classical assertions of astrology, relating to the affinities between man and wife. Astrologers declare that in the horoscopes of the spouses, there are similar positions of the sun, moon, and even of certain planets like Venus and Mars. To verify this, Jung obtained abundant material from different astrologers he knew, material that contained the birth dates of 180 married couples. Next, he calculated the horoscopes of these 360 people, and checked to see if the astrological tradition was confirmed. The result was more than he had expected: the expected relationships were flagrant and it seemed that they could not simply be attributed to some singularity or a stroke of luck. Thus astrology had a brilliant confirmation.

Rather surprised at the outcome, Jung wanted to be totally certain. He began the experiment again and assembled 220 new married couples. This time however, the result was much less clear. Obstinate, Jung gathered a third group of 83 couples. It was a catastrophe! This time, there was no more resemblance between the spouses than between groups of perfect strangers.

This discouraging succession of experiments caused Jung to reflect. He imagined that there had been a breakdown in the laws of nature, particularly in the laws of chance, such as they are usually taught.[11] He followed this by elaborating a theory that seemed to him to permit elimination of this contradiction. In psychology and elsewhere, this theory has had much reverberation. It is in fact rather ambitious, for beyond simple psychological explanation, it also claims to be a theory of the relationships between man's psyche and the universe.

Chance with direction

Jung established an immediate connection between his experimental misadventure and certain work published by Professor Rhine, an American studying telepathy. Rhine believed that he had demonstrated the role of the subject's psychological attitude in the production of results in telepathy. In experiments on guessing cards, for example, Rhine claimed that if the experiment was prolonged, the best subjects ended up guessing completely by chance, while at the beginning, their results could only—according to Rhine—be understood as a kind of as-yet unexplainable precognition. Rhine concluded that because this occurred their interest decreased, and because fatigue prevented them from maintaining their attention to the end.

But Rhine went even further. He believed that he had demonstrated that a person's a priori attitude towards the problems of telepathy influenced the value of the results. He gathered together two groups, and in the first, put only individuals hostile to telepathy; in the second group, all were favorably disposed to it. Rhine stated that the results of the former were so poor that it seemed as if they had decided as a group to intentionally guess incorrectly. On the other hand, those favorable to telepathy furnished encouraging results.

Jung gave a similar interpretation to the more or less good results obtained in his astrological experiment. His own interest, he said, had progressively diminished. If at the beginning, "it happened that my statistical research yielded precisely the results expected by astrological tradition, it seemed as if the statistical material had been almost manipulated and arranged in order to simulate a positive result."[12]

What did he mean exactly? He thought that a researcher particularly "motivated" by the desire to obtain a certain result, is instinctively—or rather unconsciously—led to gather material that will be found to confirm his theory. But this is, to be sure, a scientifically fallacious result. For the researcher who is satisfied with the initial experiment and who rests on his laurels will see the results of subsequent experiments disappear along with his interest. This is because the psyche that "is projected into things and animates them" is as if it were asleep.

And this is for Jung the occasion to show us that his position in regards to astrology is quite different than what he seemed to adopt after a superficial analysis. He found himself, he says, in the position of many astrologers. "If astrologers were more concerned with scientifically justifying astrological prediction with statistics, they would have discovered long ago that their statements rest on oscillating bases. The same thing would probably have happened to them as happened to me: they would have found a hidden reciprocal connivance *(heimliche gegenseitige konnivenz)* between the material and psychic state of the astrologer."

Jung thus refused all scientific reality to astrology, because of inconsistent and unstable results. In this way, he seems to have adopted a completely rationalistic attitude. But he troubles us a little with the strange explanation he gives for the instability of the results. His "unconscious research" for a material conforming to our psychological expectation contains something truly disturbing for a mind used to the methods of classical logic and scientific experimentation. How will Jung justify this "hidden, reciprocal connivance" between the mind and the nature that this mind seeks to explore? What is the mechanism that he proposes for it?

A universe of coincidences

Jung explains how, in his opinion, this thing is possible. According to him, science had until very recently been based uniquely on the law of causality. The rule was, *there is no effect without a cause.* Thus, for example, there was the law of weight: bodies fell because of the earth's gravitational pull. The law of causality also states that there is a *constant* relationship between cause and effect. As the physicist Jeans explains it, in a whimsical way, "If I put a vessel full of water in a burning oven it is possible that the water would change into ice. It is not statistically impossible but ... it would nonetheless be a miracle."

This is why the disconcerting problems posed by contemporary science lead Jung to remark: "The results of modern physics shake this absolute law of nature and give it only a relative validity."[13] To explain the laws of nature then, there would have to be other possible principles than those of causality. Jung gives the name of *synchronicity* to one of these principles.

The man of science says that there is no smoke without fire. Undoubtedly, answers Jung, but what proves to us that smoke always comes from fire? Could not their concomitant presence be due sometimes to a simple coincidence?

In nature, synchronicity would be a different world, one at the margin of the one we know. In this curious world, there would be effects without causes. Encounters between two events would be produced in time and space that would not be linked by physical relationships, but which would have an "analogical psychological signification."

In order to demonstrate his rather science-fiction-like theory, Jung cites a case of synchronicity that he witnessed. The psychoanalysis of one of his patients was not progressing. One day when this woman's unconscious was exhibiting a manifest hostility, Jung, no longer knowing what to try, said to her: "Well, tell me what you dreamed about last night."

"I dreamed about a beetle," said the woman. At precisely that moment, they heard a noise against the window: it was a beautiful golden beetle that was trying to get into the room. The woman was so struck by it that all her resistances fell, and Jung was able to successfully carry on the treatment.

Thus, declares Jung, "synchronicity is a physically determined relativity of time and space."[14] And finally, he hopes to arrive at a kind of unitary theory of the relationship between nature and unconscious phenomena. From this, he hoped to find an explanation for all the strange psychological phenomena that presently defied science, phenomena like the intermittent appearance of the archetypes of the collective unconscious, the moments when the mind seems to apprehend the future, and especially astrological prediction.

Perhaps Jung's attitude toward astrology will now be understood. In his estimation, it is clear that it is not a science, and that it could not be the study of the physical action of the planets on man. And if he admits that astrologers might predict the future, he does not think that the planets play an important role in the prediction. He compares the astrologer to a seer who has visions of the future, and whose mind works exactly like that of people who have a gift for telepathy.

"My intention has often been poorly understood. I did not undertake an astrological study of marriage, but rather an essay on the behavior of numbers to which a certain autonomy can be attributed. In situations that manifest an archetype (and astrology is one of these), figures often correspond to an emotional expectation, under the influence of an organizing factor."[15]

Jung offers another anecdote as proof of this. At the time he was pursuing his research on marriage, he organized a large dinner party at his home. His assistant was responsible for the seating arrangement, according to custom and precedence. She did it carefully, but at the last minute, an important and unexpected guest arrived. A suitable p to us to be sure that we truly have an effective process.

arrangment, according to custom and precedence. She did it carefully, but at the last minute, an important and unexpected guest arrived. A suitable place had to be found for him, but it would upset the arrangement of the table. Somewhat distracted, the assistant quickly made the necessary adjustments. "When we were seated," relates Jung, "it happened that with his immediate neighbors, this guest formed four pseudo-marriages that conformed to astrological tradition. I must add the for a long time, my collaborator had been working on the astrological aspects of marriage, and was completely familiar with its principles. She also knew the horoscopes of each of the people in question. In her preoccupation, she did not have time think, and thus her unconscious had complete latitude to arrange these couples."[16] In short, in her desire to make the last guest comfortable, she unconsciously had recourse to the astrological affinities whose rules she knew.

Thus, according to Jung, the mind can become detached from rational evidence—especially in states of strong emotion—and penetrate a world of categories other than those of space and time. It also happens sometimes that an astrologer pierces someone's character or foresees a future event. Astrologers without astrology: this seems to be the basis of the master of Zurich, whose philosophical doctrine rejoins Leibnitz's famous conception of preestablished harmonies.

Between the immanent will of the Chaldean god-lights and the doctrine of synchronicity there are forty centuries of effort by the best astrologers to explain the nature of astral influence. The very diversity of opinion and the vivacity of the discussion show how far the problem is from being resolved. It can at least be noted that these efforts are to the astrologer's credit.

While jealously guarding his secrets, might astrology be gifted with a mystical power to unveil the future? But have all these authors not put the cart before the horse, have they not wrongly considered as resolved a much more important factor that the *how* and *why* of astral influence: the very existence of this influence? It is time to answer this question.

Notes

1. R. Abellio, "L'Astrologie, science, art ou sagesse (wisdom)" in *Janus: 8*, pp. 132–135.

2. Letter from Kepler to his mentor Malin (1598), cited by Strauss in *Die Astrologie Keplers.*

3. *Paul Choisnard, La Loi d'hérédité astrale,* 1919. Cf. also my experimental criticism of this "law" in my paper "L'hérédité astrale," *Las Cahiers astrologiques:98,* 1962, pp. 135–143.

4. Bouché-Leclerq, *op. cit.*

5. *Cited by J. Hieroz: L'Astrologie Selon Morin de Ville-franche,* Omnium litteraire, 1962, p. 12.

6. In his books *Le Probléme de la Destinée. NRF, 1928.*

7. *André* Barbault, *Traité Pratique d'Astrologie,* Le Seuil, 1961.

8. C. G. Jung, *Complete Works,* vol. 10, 1964.

9. *Astrologie moderne:12* December, 1964, pp. 2, 4.

10. His personal contribution to this work is entitled: *Synchronizität als ein Prinzip akausaler Zusammenhänge.* Rascher Verlag Zurich, 1952. Published in English by Routledge and Kegan Paul Ltd. (London): *Synchronicity: An Acausal Connecting Principle,* 1972.

11. This is not however, the opinion of statisticians who think that Jung's mathematical interpretation is not correct. I also expressed this conclusion as early as 1958 in a letter to Dr. H. Bender, professor of psychology (Freiburg University, Germany) when my opinion on this subject was requested.

12. Cf. Jung, *Op. cit.*

13. Jung, *Op. cit.*

14. Jung, *Op. cit.*

15. *Zeitschrift fur Parapsychologie und Grenzgebiete der Psychologie I,* no. 2/3, 1957, Francke-Verlag, Berne, p. 92.

16. Jung, *Op. cit.*

CHAPTER 5
Science or fiction?

Do astrological predictions correspond to reality? There are different ways of approaching this question. It can be judged by common sense, or through the use of adequate scientific methods. "Common sense being the best distributed thing in the world" (as Descartes said), everyone feels that he is qualified to give an opinion on astrology through the interpretation of his horoscope. But this is a poor method, as we shall see later: people are not objective when reading their own horoscope.

A procedure used by many astrologers consists in illustrating their assertions with the publications of horoscopes of famous people. Let us try to enter this game by using astrology's cornerstone, the signs of the zodiac. With the aid of celebrities born under the same sign, let us see if certain characteristic constants become apparent in the lives of these people, as the astrologers declare.

Famous examples

It is not difficult to make a "mini-dictionary" of notables born under each of the twelve signs. Proceeding without preconceived ideas, one is struck by the strange groupings contained by these lists. We will only give three signs as examples: Libra, Capricorn and Virgo.

Libra (September 23–October 22)

The sign supposedly confers the qualities of moderation, equilibrium, urbanity and sincerity of feelings. Let us mention several well-known Libras. First of all in literature: the poetic sensitivity of Lamartine, born on October 21, 1790[1], gives a point to astrology that is immediately lost when it is learned that Nietzsche, the philosopher of the will to power, was born under the same sign, on October 15, 1844. Could there be a character less stable and less conciliatory than that of this genial but neurotic visionary? In politics, astrologers are correct in noting that Gandhi, the apostle of nonviolence born on October 1, 1869, certainly seems to possess the characteristics of his sign. But they silently pass over the fact that the sinister Himmler, the *Reichsfuürer* of the S.S. was also a Libra, born on October 7, 1900. Among the kings of France, Louis XIII, born on September 27, 1601, and called the Just, does indeed seem to have been a humane, amicable, and sentimental prince. But on the other hand, his illustrious father Henry IV, born with his ascendant in the same sign, had a completely different temperament. Among actors, the relationship between the Venusian Brigitte Bardot, born on September 28, 1934, and the comic Jacques Tati born on October 9, 1908, is not at all evident. Finally, is it not surprising that a stunt man like Gil Delamare was born on October 14, 1924, under a constellation that supposedly confers a "small amount of energy?"

Capricorn (December 21–January 19)

Let us recall that natives of Capricorn are supposedly cold, ambitious, phlegmatic, and reflective individuals who have a rather difficult time in their social contacts. These qualities can be applied to Stalin, born on January 3, 1880. But it is difficult to say they apply to Marshall Joffre, a placid, jovial, and good man.[2] It is even more difficult in the case of the great scientist Louis Pasteur, who is universally known for his compassion. However, a truculent and dynamic actor like Pierre Brasseur was born on December 22 with the sun and ascendant in Capricorn. The dynamic entertainer Suzy Delair was born right in the middle of the sign, on December 31, 1916. The astrologers tell us the "climbing goat" can also be important for the natives of Capricorn, and they are happy to cite Maurice Herzog, the conqueror of Anapurna, who was born on January 15, 1919. Fine. But a psychological world separates the mountain climber from an impressionist painter like Cezanne, whose birthday was January 19, 1839—a man who spent his time contemplating nature from the doorstep of his cottage, and not exploring it with his knapsack on his back. Or there is Utrillo, the damned painter of Montmartre, whose passion for painting was rivaled only by his passion for alcohol. Also, the opposition between the bohemian life of a Utrillo and the rigorous life of a Pasteur is, to say the least, striking. Finally, note that Richard Nixon (born January 9, 1913) and the famous cellist Pablo Casals (born December 30, 1876) are both Capricorns; but it is hard to see similarities between them.

Virgo (August 23–September 22)

The sign confers on the subject a modest, prudent, irresolute, methodic, almost maniacal character. In the gallery of historical personages, we can note—with the astrologers—that Louis XVI was born on August 23, 1754, and that the irresoluteness of his character was one of the causes of his downfall. But Louis XIV, one of his illustrious predecessors on the throne of France, was also born in Virgo, on September 5, 1638. The Sun King had many mistresses, and loved to be surrounded by courtisans from the time he arose until he went to bed. For him, being a king was "the most wonderful trade in the world." The unflaggingly willful and authoritarian Richelieu was also born in Virgo (September 9, 1585), as was the revolutionary fanatic Saint-Just (August 25, 1767), who voted for the death of Louis XVI. But let us leave history. The romantic poet Theophile Gautier—who wore to the openings of Hugo's Hernani a suit so odd that it has remained famous to this day—does not seem to have had many affinities with the Virgo type; nevertheless he was born on August 30, 1873. It is the same for the author of *Ubu Roi*, Alfred Jarry (September 8, 1873); or even the energetic actor Jean-Louis Barrault, born on September 8, 1910, with the sun and the ascendant in Virgo. Finally, what common point could the astrologer find between the following Virgos (listed in alphabetical order): Césare Borgia, Chateaubriand, Colbert, Cuvier, and Ivan the Terrible?

Rather than to Capricorn, Libra, or Virgo, the above-named personages could be psychologically attributed to many signs other than the ones they were born in. Nietzsche the Libra would make a good Capricorn, and the Capricorn Suzy Delair would be a very acceptable Libra. Jean-Louis Barrault could have been a Leo, a "spectacular" sign, as could have Louis XIV. Gil Delamare should have perhaps been born in Aries—a more dynamic sign—and Jerry in Scorpio, for his biting satiric writings.

The astrologers respond: no individual is a pure type and the whole of the horoscope must always be taken into account. There are, however, astrologers who publish such galleries of portraits and who affirm the presence of a universe that is psychologically common to those born in the same sign. Very often, their objection turns against them. The timorous Louis XVI is certainly a Virgo, but in the first house, that of character, he has the planet Mars, the planet of courage, energy, and the spirit of decision. These qualities however, seem to have been entirely lacking from the unfortunate sovereign.

The truth is that the procedure which consists in proving astrology by famous examples is not satisfactory. We are convinced that the little experiment just undertaken provides neither elements *for* or *against* astrology. The establishment of such galleries is an unusable means of arriving at an objective opinion on the value of the horoscope.

The case of identical twins

Let us push our analysis a little further. There should exist a simple and direct means of finding out if what the horoscope says is true. It would suffice to examine the destiny of several pairs of twins. For two identical horoscopes, the destiny ought to be identical. Does this happen? Long ago Cicero exclaimed, "Did all of those who died at the Battle of Cannes have the same horoscope?" And here is the opinion of a contemporary astronomer, Paul Couderc: "If astrology were true, twins ought to have the same destiny, and especially identical twins, whose hereditary stock is identical. But since Antiquity, the dissemblance of their destinies has been fatal to astrology."[3]

The problem is perhaps somewhat more complicated and more nuanced than unconditional adversaries to astrology might think. In any case, astrologers deny the validity of this definitive condemnation. They state that identical twins—those who come from one egg cell—very frequently have strangely parallel destinies. The experiments of Professor Kallman of the Psychiatric Institute of New York certainly seems to confirm this. He examined 27,000 pairs of identical twins and concluded: "Every individual carries in him a clock that is regulated at his birth and that predetermines notably illnesses and accidents." Kallman cites as well the case of a set of twins separated at birth, raised in different adoptive homes, and who both chose a military career, retiring at the rank of colonel.

The famous Swiss astrologer, Krafft, patiently consulted the archives of the civil registry in his country. In his *Traité d'astro-biologie,* he cites some disturbing cases. Twins born in Plainpalais on June 6, 1914, for example, one at 7:45 and the other at 7:50 in the morning, both died at the age of two months of gastro-enteritis. Two others born in Geneva on February 11, 1876, at 2:00 P.M. and 2:15 P.M., both committed suicide by drowning at the age of forty-six, one three months after the other. Other twins, born in Saone-et-Loire on May 11, 1835, at 1:00 P.M., both died at a very advanced age, one at 90 years and the other at 91.

For his part, Dr. Allendy has pointed out the case of the Chanteau brothers, born in Nantes on May 18, 1874, one at 11:30 and the second at 11:45. The resemblance between them was extraordinary. They drew successive numbers in the lottery and married twin sisters on the same day. Let us also recall the story of the twins of La Réole, the Faucher brothers, César and Constantin, who were born in 1759. Their lives were completely parallel. Both lawyers, they joined the army during the Revolution and were both named generals after having been wounded in the Vendée. And their deaths were also identical: they were executed on the same day in 1815 by the English for having rejoined Napoleon during the Hundred Days.

These coincidences are not the result of chance but neither do we need the planets to explain them. Identical twins are the identical reproduction of one being. Drawing on the same hereditary stock, they possess the same aptitudes, the same characteristic and morbid tendencies. Psychological and medical literature abounds with observations of this or that psychic or mental problem which is almost simultaneously repeated during the life of identical twins. To this is added the narrow psychological and educational links formed between twins from childhood on. Their peculiar situation— which is often reinforced by parents who enjoy pushing the resemblance to the maximum—naturally leads the children, once they are adults, to pursue the same careers. It is therefore the social milieu and heredity that must be invoked here, and not the influence of the planets.

In truth, there are many contradictory cases. Until the advent of modern obstetric techniques, twins had a poor chance of survival. Very often, one would die at birth while the other, having weathered the difficult storm of birth, would live to an advanced age. Multiple births present the same problems to mothers. Quadruplets and quintuplets often leave only one survivor. Even in an exceptional case when all five quintuplets survive, their destiny can be very different. Thus in the case of the Dionne sisters, one, who had taken religious vows, died early, while the other four are still living.

There is also a French case, reported recently in the press under the title: "Five were born, four survive, but now there are only three." During the darkest days of the war, in the space of an hour five children were born in the home of Émile Dupuis, a miner. The last to be born, a girl, died of suffocation, but four boys lived: Pierre, Jacques, Jean, and André. Pierre, the strongest of the four, died a year later. The others are in good health. Like their father, Jacques and Jean are mine workers. André, preferring to work above the ground, became a mason. Of the three surviving quints, he is the only one that is married.

The element of chance, upon which astrological prediction might focus, often intervenes in different ways for twins. A recent news item reports that when a shot was fired on the second floor of an apartment building, the bullet penetrated the ceiling and killed one of a pair of twins sleeping side by side in their crib on the third floor; his brother was unhurt, however. Elsewhere, the criminal files mention the case of a twin who was obsessed by the perpetual presence of a double at his side, and eventually murdered him with a knife.

The examination of the character and destiny of identical twins does not appear to be a valid proof of planetary influence. It is rather the expression of another truth that two Nobel Prize winners in chemistry—Watson and Crick—have demonstrated: the genetic code acts like a program on an IBM card, and in a way, it is the individual's personality that is programmed. The programs of twins produce similar personalities, but not similar destinies.

Astro twins

The cases of fraternal twins, that is to say children born on the same day but from separate eggs, are hardly more decisive on the "astral" plane.

But there is a more interesting study: the examination of the character and destiny of two individuals who are *not linked by any bonds of kinship,* individuals who are born on the same day, even at the same hour. If there is a striking analogy between the two, this time it is impossible to invoke heredity to explain the resemblances. In his imaged language, Krafft talks of "astro twins." Disturbing parallels are often discovered in the lives of these subjects. During our statistical investigations, we have discovered one of these. Two champion bicycle racers—Paul Chocque, born on July 14, 1910, and Léon Level, born on July 12, 1910—met the same fate. It was in 1936 that they achieved their fame, the former.winning the Bordeaux-Paris section and the latter two mountain sections of the Tour de France races. Later in their careers, both decided to become motorcycle racers. Level was killed when he fractured his skull on the Parc de Princes track in March, 1949, and Paul Choque died in September of the same year from a similar injury on the same track.

There is also a classic example that every astrological manual fervently recalls. It is the case of King George III of England and one of his subjects, an iron merchant named Samuel Hemmings. Both were supposedly born at the same hour on June 4, 1738. Their two lives bear witness to a startling chronological concordance. It is said that they were married on the same day, and that Hemmings took over his father's business on the day that George III ascended to the throne. Finally, they both died when they were over eighty years old, and on the same day, of course (January 29, 1820). If it were based on precise facts, this example alone could doubtless be an argument in favor of astral influence. For this reason we have sought exact and verifiable references. Unfortunately, they could not be obtained. We could not even discover the name of the first astrologer—who was probably an Englishman—to mention this example, and one can certainly wonder to what degree his imagination entered into his assertions!

Krafft made a collection of "astro twins." He had discovered his own "astro twin" in the person of another astrologer named Otto von Bressensdorf. And in his *Traité d'astrobiologie,* he relates that one day he felt the effects of a serious and inexplicable fit of depression. Some time later, Krafft learned that von Bressensdorf had committed suicide at the precise moment that he had felt overcome by desperation. His "twin" was no more. Among the cases of "astro twins," Krafft cites that of a man and a woman born on November 24, 1836, at 4:00 P.M., one in the Swiss town of Corsier and the other in Geneva. They died at an advanced age within eighteen months of each other, the man on November 19, 1920, and the woman on March 3, 1922. Krafft also gives the names of twenty-six men born at about the same time who were all killed during the First World War. It is also interesting to note that two of Hitler's well-known ministers, Hermann Goering and Alfred Rosenberg, were born on the same day—January 12, 1893—and were both executed on October 16, 1946, having been condemned to death at Nuremburg.

There are, however, numerous astro twins that present great differences both in character and destiny.

Here are a few contemporary examples. Raymond Cartier, the publisher of the French magazine *Paris-Match,* was born the same day as the heart surgeon, Dr. Monod. Yvon Bourges, a former French government minister, was born on the same day as the writer Frederic Dard, the father of the whimsical Inspector San Antonio. Wilfrid Baumgartner, the former French Finance Minister, was born on the same day as Anatole Litvak, the film director. Another former minister, Lucien Paye, was born on June 28, 1907, as was the explorer, Paul-Émile Victor. The writer Kleber Haedens and the actor Jean Marais both came into the world on December 11, 1913. And finally, let us note that the great comic French actor, Jules Raimu, who died in 1946, was born at precisely the same time (3:00 A.M.) as the writer-minister Abel Bonnard, who died in 1968, and only twenty-four hours separated their birth. Raimu was born on December 18, 1883, and Bonnard on the 19th.[4]

Each of us can participate in the game of astro twins. The author of these lines has not failed to do so. During the course of his research, he has noted the name and situation of those born the same day as he (November 13, 1928). There is among them a former captain of the French National Rugby Team, Jean-Pierre Saux, a chronic alcoholic committed to the Sainte-Anne Hospital, and a "small time swindler" who was briefly mentioned one day in the newspaper. And it is not without pleasure that it was learned that Princess Grace of Monaco was born on November 12, 1928, that is to say, under almost the same heavens.[5] The problem of astro twins when considered to furnish proof of the validity of the horoscope, is thus very difficult to resolve. Above all, an impartial investigation must be carried on, taking into account all cases that are encountered without seeking to know if such cases confirm or deny astral influence. Then the probability of appearance that is due to chance must be evaluated for the number of similar cases. For this, it is first of all necessary to establish the precise limits of the observed coincidences: Within these limits, can two *almost* identical birth dates that correspond to two *almost* similar destinies be considered as proof? Finally and especially, the probability of appearance of cases of astro twins with analogous destinies must be calculated as a function of (a) the total number of cases of pairs examined and (b) the occurrence of a similar event during their lifetimes.

Let us explain this further: the astrologer Krafft congratulates himself for having found twenty or so individuals born on the same

day and who died in the First World War. But alas, a simple calculation shows that such a phenomenon is *normal*. Let us estimate—and
such a figure is probably well below the actual figure—that 100,000
French and German soldiers of the class of 1913 (born in 1893) were
killed on the battlefield during the war. This would mean that approximately 270 male children born on the same day would have
been killed in the War. More precisely, every hour of the 365 days of
1893, there were approximately ten children born in France and
Germany who were assured the same tragic destiny. It would suffice
to examine the birth records of any French community to be assured
of this sad statistical reality. On every page, like a leitmotif in the
margin of the birth records, there is inscribed: "died on the field of
battle." In other words, one is obliged to state that the "disturbing
cases" are, as a statistical necessity, found to be in much greater
number than common sense would lead one to believe, without it
thereby being possible to find any argument in favor of the horoscope. To be sure, a systematic investigation of the circumstances of
the lives of a hundred individuals born on the same day and at the
same time might provide us with more definitive conclusions on the
problem posed. But what has been the existence of dozens of children who came into the world with the same horoscope as Adolph
Hitler, Charles DeGaulle or John F. Kennedy?

Statistical Studies

Thus neither famous examples nor astro twins can manage to definitively establish a proof for or against the reality of the horoscope. It
is necessary to apply more rigorous methods, and we have just
evoked the use of statistics. This modern scientific tool can be used
in a systematic way to determine the value of astrological laws. It
has been rightly said that the principal aim of science is to establish
categories within the phenomena of nature. Astrology's categories
can be the empirical formulas that we reviewed in Chapter three
above. Rather than globally judging the validity of the horoscope,
one can try to dismantle the mechanism, verifying one by one the
laws upon which it rests. Proceeding in this way, a method whose
effectiveness has been shown in all the physical sciences can be
employed. Here is a prosaic example. When you think that your car
is not running properly, you take it to a mechanic. In order to examine the engine, the mechanic is obliged to check the condition of
the parts of which it is composed. We have doubts on the validity of

the horoscope. The best procedure is therefore to examine each of the astrological factors of which it is composed by putting them to the statistical test.

Let us isolate a precise astronomical factor: the presence of the sun in the sign of Aries in a horoscope, for example. This configuration corresponds to a *part of destiny:* "Predisposition to adventure, to accidents, to struggle, fights, and rivalry," writes an astrologer. Then we can examine several hundred people who have clearly shown a disposition to adventure. One can use for example, the *Dictionnaire des Généraux de la Révolution et de l'Empire,*[6] noting the sign in which these personages were born. There are thus two possibilities: either the astrological rule is correct, and the number of generals born in the sign of Aries will be so great that the number of births in this region of the heavens cannot be explained by chance; or the birthdays of the generals in question will be dispersed almost uniformly in each of the twelve signs, and Aries will only have its average share of the total. In the latter case, the astrological law concerning the destiny of natives of Aries is not confirmed. With the necessary patience, and information, one could theoretically test the reliability of each to the cogs of the horoscope by following the same procedure.

One fact is worthy of attention: it was not men of science who first had the idea of applying statistical methods to astrology, but rather the astrologers themselves. At the beginning of this century, Paul Choisnard had the great merit of advocating the use of great numbers of examples in order to demonstrate the influence of the planets. He undertook several studies, of which the results favorable to the horoscope were published in *Preuves et bases de l'astrologie scientifique.*[7] In the next generation, Krafft took up the flame and assembled an impressive accounting favorable to astrology in his monumental *Traite d'astrobiologie.*[8]

But the calculation of probabilities needs delicate handling. There is the well-known statement of Disraeli, for whom "statistics are the most serious form of deception." Occasionally, one also hears that "you can make statistics say anything and everything." In fact, they are only a form of deception to the extent that one does not know how to use them. It is a technique that must be assimilated, and the misunderstanding of "the laws of probability" has led to many errors in science by researchers of good faith. Choisnard and his successors, for example, were assuredly men of good faith. But were they able to avoid the numerous stumbling blocks in the calculation of probabilities? It is the obligation of the man of science to find out.

Pitfalls to avoid

In a work published in 1955, *L'Influence des Astres, étude critique et expérimentale,*[9] we presented a complete analysis of the statistical works of Choisnard and of Krafft. We would refer the reader interested in the details to this volume. We must be content here with a few extracted examples in order to illustrate the present concern. Outside of the statistical technique itself, two pitfalls in astrology must be avoided.

The first is to take for an astrological law what is only an astronomical one. It is disappointing to note that Choisnard has committed this error on several occasions. This negates one of the author's most successful propositions: the "law of ascendants for superior minds." Having collected the horoscopes of a great number of people famed for their exceptional intelligence, Choisnard asserts that their ascendants were not distributed evenly among the twelve signs of the zodiac. He observes a noticeable grouping of these ascendants in the triple zone of Libra-Aquarius-Gemini,"with an extension into the neighboring signs of Virgo and Scorpio on the side of Libra . . . the signs of Sagittarius, Capricorn, Pisces, Aries, and Taurus [however] possess very few ascendants of superior minds . . . ; thus the ascendant marks a kind of map of human faculties."[10] In reality, the signs of the zodiac in France do not have the same duration of passage in the ascendant, and those that have been noted by Choisnard as the most frequent for higher minds are quite simply the most frequent for everyone. It is an error quite similar to one that might be committed by a sociologist who, noting that in Paris the number of white people of higher intelligence is much greater than that of black people, who conclude that whites are more intelligent than blacks. For in Paris, the white population is in an enormous majority.

The second pitfall to be avoided is to take a demographic law for an astrological law. One of Krafft's principal affirmations is that "the sun's position has an effect on musical aptitude," and this is an illustration of this type of error. Krafft took from Rieman's music dictionary the names of 2,817 musicians and, for each of them, noted the birth sign. The final result showed a preponderance of musicians to be born in the sign of Taurus. Governed by Venus, the planet of the arts, Taurus is certainly a sign of artistic tendency. Krafft seemed to have demonstrated an astrological law. Unfortunately, he had not taken into account a demographic factor of births. In central Europe, the distribution of births throughout the months of the year is not even. More children are born in the spring than in the winter. It follows that the number of little Taurus born in May is always greater than that of little Sagittarius born in December. The births of musicians only obeyed this demographic law. The artistic influence attributed by Krafft to the sign of Taurus was without foundation. Paul Couderc, the astronomer, who has analyzed in detail Krafft's statistics, adds that "musicians are born by chance throughout the year. No sign or fraction of a zodiacal sign either favors or opposes them."[11]

It happens however, that error is not discernible, that a law proposed by an astrologer does not destroy itself. Must we be content with this to believe in the influence of the planets? Let us recall that a scientific fact must be a "fact reproducible at will." If the law proposed by the astrologer truly corresponds to a natural phenomenon, any researcher must be able to prove it again. Choisnard, for example, studied the effect of the planets on health. For him, there was "manifest proof that man does not meet death under just any heaven." He collected two hundred observations of death that demonstrated that the malefic Mars and Saturn are two and three times more often in conjunction with the birth Sun at the moment of death than at other moments."Although it was a rather small sample, the statistical method was correctly executed. We thus sought to check this assertion by assembling a much greater number of deaths than in Choisnard's sample, in order to be certain in this domain. The study examined 7,482 comparisons between the horoscope of birth and that of death: the supposed negative influence of Mars and Saturn was revealed to be nonexistent.[12] For his part, Couderc performed a counter-experiment with Mars alone. His conclusion, based on the examination of four thousand deaths, is in agreement with ours: "The statistics have a result that conforms to the laws of chance," he writes.[13] There is therefore hardly any doubt that Choisnard's good faith was surprised by some stroke of luck that was never again repeated.

Scientific observation

Astrologers are poor defenders of their own cause. But this does not automatically prove that their cause is a bad one. The astrologer is mistaken about his statistics, but in spite of everything, there may be something true in astrology. Scientists have taken over for astrologers, and with the aid of statistics, have tried to verify astrological laws. Such is the case with the American astronomer, Allen Hynek. He collected the birthdates of the *American Men of Science* members, a listing that includes all of America's talented researchers. Nothing distinguished the birthdates of these scientists from those of their fellow men, however: they were found in each of the signs of the zodiac, obeying only the above-mentioned demographic law. The result is no better if one separates—as Hynek did—the chemists from the physicists, the psychologists from the surgeons, and so on. Farnsworth, another researcher, wanted to judge the validity of another proposition often found in astrological manuals: Libra would supposedly favor an individual's artistic predisposition. Farnsworth found no correlation between the birthdates of more than two thousand famous musicians and painters. In our own research, we have demonstrated through the analysis of the birthdates of more than twenty-five thousand celebrities that there is no relationship between these individuals' personal vocation and their birth signs, whether it be the sun sign or the ascendant.[14] Thus the 1,995 generals from the French Revolution through the First Empire have their share of natives of Aries and no more. A study of a group of subway ticket-takers would have given the same result. Thus chance preferred that professional boxers be more often Cancers, the sign of the dreaming mood, than Aries, the impetuous Mars.[15]

We were interested enough in this to cast the horoscopes of two thousand children from metropolitan Paris who died at an early age. There was no significant result.[16] The house of the aggressive and bloody Mars was calculated for the births of 623 famous murderers (for which we were obligingly permitted to consult the records of the Paris Palace of Justice). It should have been expected that Mars be in the eighth house, that of death, or else the twelfth house, that of trials and prisons. But there is nothing of the kind; in the horoscopes of these 623 murderers, Mars showed no preference at all, and was found just as often in any of the twelve houses.[17]

But let us not try the patience of the reader. Let us only refer him to the specialized works mentioned. Let us only state that to the present day, no law of classical astrology has been demonstrated with the aid of statistics, whether by astrologers or scientists.

Impossibilities

Is this so surprising, the scientists ask? The horoscope is an anachronism that is incompatible with the present state of knowledge. A

94

horosocope based on the moment of conception would perhaps be less categorically rejected by the scholar; but for the astrologer, it is the moment of birth that counts above all. Perhaps if he only analyzed character and did not enter into prediction he would have a less poor reputation; but the astrologer predicts the future. How can this "delayed determinism" be justified, this doctrine that programs the important dates of our existence according to a fugitive configuration of the heavens?

Of all the scientists, astronomers have the most reason to attack astrology. For them, there is no doubt: the foundations of astrology have no valid basis. While astronomers have numerous objections, we shall only consider two of them here. The first disputes the zodiac, and bears on the phenomenon of the precession of the equinoxes. The second is concerned with the inclination of the ecliptic, and tends to demonstrate the inanity of the doctrine of houses and even of the ascendant.

The precession of the equinoxes

An important phenomenon is hidden in this at once poetic and enigmatic term. The location of the constellations in the heavens did not appear to us the same two thousand years ago as it does today. What has happened? The earth turns on its axis like a top. Now the axis of this top, while turning on itself, also slowly describes a cone around the vertical. And this exceedingly slow movement is the precession of equinoxes.[18] This discovery was made by Hipparchus, in the second century B.C. The consequence is that in the last two thousand years, the constellations have moved back a sign. In Hipparchus' time, when a Greek child was born in the month of August, the sun was in the constellation of Leo. Today, when a child is born in August, the sun is crossing the constellation of Cancer; the astrologer however, continues to attribute the newborn with the qualities of the king of beasts and not the familial ones of Cancer. The passing centuries have mixed-up and shifted the zodiacal influences. Imagine a motion picture in which the sound progressively changes in relation to the image, because of a technical error. You would see the hero fall to the ground mortally wounded, but would only hear the report of the rifle thirty seconds later. For the astronomer, the precession of the equinoxes is the condemnation of astrology, and a condemnation from which there is no appeal.

The astrologers, of course, do not agree with this, and in fact, they find the objection easy to refute. The constellation crossed by the sun plays no role, they say. What matters is the sign. The precession of the equinoxes does not prevent spring from beginning on March 22, the day of the equinox. It is the same for the influence of the sun: it is immutable. It matters little that behind it, the constellations change position, with an imperceptible and majestic slowness.

This explanation is not very clear. For in this case the sign would only be mathematical convention without consistence. But the history of astrology indicates that on the contrary, it was the constellation that mattered for the ancients. "When the moon shall enter the pincers of Scorpio, there will be an invasion of locusts," states a Chaldean omen. The constellation's influence has given the tone of the prediction. As Couderc remarks, it is as if by chance that "the virtues of each sign express very precisely the supposed qualities of the mythical animal that today inhabits the preceding zodiacal region.[19] This complicates the astrologer's defense. He must admit that a kind of remanence has impregnated the influence held by the sign during the preceding centuries. But what was the influence in even earlier times, twenty centuries before Hipparchus, for example? One falls inexorably into a vicious circle that renders doubtful the influence of the signs of the zodiac, such as it is conceived by contemporary astrologers.

The inclination of the ecliptic

This phenomenon radically deprives children born above the polar circle (66 degrees latitude) of a "normal"horoscope. Because of the inclination of the ecliptic on the celestial equator, above this latitude it can happen that "the ecliptic coincides with the horizon and crosses no houses."[20] Think of the midnight sun, which neither rises nor sets. The horoscope has become a monster, like a headless animal or an automobile without wheels. What is the fate that awaits children born in Siberia, in Lapland, in Alaska, in Finland, and so on? Born in a less septentrional latitude, the Chaldean astrologer did not need to envisage a solution to this problem; today however, such a solution is urgently needed.

Here then are many serious theoretical objections to astrology; but they are only theoretical. They shake neither the faith of the astrologer, nor that of his clients. Certainly they do not disturb them more than the disappointing results of statistical investigations. Since astrology is not necessarily of the same nature as science, criticizing it solely from this criteria might seem to be a mistake, or even an injustice: the horoscope is an organic whole, say the astrologers, and each element has an effect on all others. To take apart one by one the factors of the birth heaven is to kill the latter's meaning. Cut a man into a hundred thousand pieces and examine each of them with diligence and care. You will never know how a whole, living man functions. "The only criteria we accept is that of efficacity," say the majority of astrologers. "Give us complete horoscopes to interpret and judge our predictions as a whole." In the same way, the ever-increasing numbers who practice mundane astrology state: "It is easy to sneer at us when we cast the horoscope of a country or of a peace treaty. But it would be more useful to see us at work. Our clientele is satisfied. For us, this is an evident proof of the validity of the horoscope. If we regularly committed errors, it is certain that no one would come for consultation. Besides, you must remember that our clients are far from being weak minds or mentally unbalanced. We are regularly consulted by those in important positions—businessmen, bankers, politicians, actors, and writers—and they are quite satisfied."

An argument based on the satisfaction and fidelity of customers seems valid a priori. If a restaurant is full every night, one might think that the fare is excellent. A pianist who draws a large crowd to each of his concerts is probably a talented musician. Thanks to the computerized horoscope, we shall judge without ambiguity if the testimony of the astrologer's clients can be compared to that of a gourmet or that of a music lover.

Notes

1. But near to the frightening and warlike Scorpio.
2. Head of the Allied Army at the end of World War I.
3. *Op. cit.*
4. Astrologers can be somewhat puzzled by this famous historical case: Abraham Lincoln and Charles Darwin were born the same day: February 12, 1809. . . .
5. According to some biographers, however, she was born in either 1929 or 1930.
6. George Six ed., Archives de la Seine.
7. Published by Chacornac, Paris, 2nd ed., 1921.
8. Published by Le grand, Paris, 1939.
9. Laboratoire d'Etude des Relations entre Rythmes Cosmiques et psychophysiologiques, Paris; see also our review in *The Skeptical Inquirer*, 2, 2, 1978 p. 118–122.
10. *Preuves et bases de l'astrologie scientifique.*

11. Couderc, *op. cit.*

12. Gauquelin, *op. cit.*

13. *Op. cit.*

14. M. and F. Gauquelin, *Statistical Tests of Zodiacal Influ ences,* Book 1 (Profession and Heredity) L.E.R.R.C.P., 1978.

15. To this the astrologers responded that the ideogram of the sign of Cancer—a reversed 6 and 9—was obviously the symbol of a fighter who kept his two arms folded over his chest to protect himself. . . .

16. "Le ciel de naissance des enfants morts en bas âge," *Les Cahiers astrologiques;* 111, 1964.

17. *L'Influence des astres* (Table of results, p. 239).

18. This movement is in the opposite direction of daily rotation.

19. *Op. cit.*, p. 62

20. Couderc, *op. cit.*

CHAPTER 6
The sign of the computer

For astrology, 1968 was a revolutionary year: the marriage between horoscope and computer was consumated. Replacement of the turbaned astrologer with a program on punched cards is a progress at least as enormous as that from the stagecoach to the interplanetary rockets; and at the same time, it provides an occasion for the rehabilitation of astrology, which had been expelled from the university for 300 years. An immense hope was born among serious researchers. Stripped of its occult trappings, astrology could finally meet science face to face, thanks to the cold objectivity of machines. It had finally reached its own "Copernican revolution."

Our story begins around the middle of 1967, inside an advertising executive's fertile head; the unexpected marriage of these two fascinating creatures—astrology and computers—was to prove itself an invaluable aid in the sale of a certain brand of laundry soap. One had only to purchase the product in question to receive one's very own "computoscope." The great success of this promotion technique convinced others that there was probably money to be made by selling "computerized horoscopes" for their own sake. Several companies were begun almost simultaneously, both in Europe and the United States. They took out copyrights to protect themselves from plagiarism; and the commercial trademarks used up practically all possible combinations of the four key words, "horoscope" and "astrology," on one hand, and "computer" and "electronics" on the other. Each company prided itself in having a famous astrologer—the best, of course—in charge of its programming. But their finances were not equal. The weaker companies were swept away in less than six months by the severe competition. Today in France, one powerful company almost exclusively controls this paradoxical market. Its financial assets appear to be considerable, and it demonstrates an astrological ambition that is the equal of its means. The *Ordinamus*[1] company has engaged the services of a well-known astrologer, "the author of 26 books, several of which have been translated into other languages." With a large advertising budget, its large ads can be found in all the daily newspapers. No doubt every reader, at one time or another, has been intrigued or irritated by advertising copy like this:

WILL MAY 3, 1980, BE IN A LUCKY
OR AN UNLUCKY PERIOD FOR YOU?

Your life is made up of evil and harmonious periods. Ordinamus will reveal them to you for the ten years to come. For the first time, your complete psycho-astrological file drawn up on an IBM computer under the supervision of the leading modern astrologer, . . .for only 120 Francs. [approx. $30.00]

or even like this:

ORDINAMUS—MUCH MORE THAN A HOROSCOPE
WHAT WILL HAPPEN IN *YOUR* LIFE?

The electronic computer accomplishes what an astrologer never could, because of the long calculations needed. Ordinamus' 360/30 computer, programmed by B . . ., the vice-president of the International Astrological Center, can cast your horoscope for the ten years to come. . . . Would you like to learn about yourself and your future in greater detail? Send the coupon. . . .

It is not the commercial or anecdotic aspect that interests us here, but rather the scientific possibility that this enterprise presents. Indeed, *Ordinamus* offers us an exceptional opportunity to test astrology—perhaps for the first time—without any bias or ambiguity. We find the best possible conditions, in fact. On the one hand, there is "the greatest astrologer of our time," and on the other a computer program in which horoscopic techniques have been digested, and over the astrologer has no control once it has been fed into the machine: the latter is particularly important. The astrologer cannot avoid a fair test, nor, in the case of failure, can he rely on sophistic hairsplitting to cover his mistakes. With the computer, the fate of the astrologer, like that of his client, is sealed in two minutes; for that is how long it takes a teleprinter to type out the character and destiny of the individual. Each electronic horoscope is thus an unequivocal piece of evidence. In passing through the computer, could astrology finally obtain the nobility so long refused it by men of science? A serious, objective and in-depth study deserved to be undertaken. And this we have done in collaboration with the well known French journal *Science et vie.*[2]

The program of a horoscope

In order for the experiment to be truly decisive, we must put all the trump cards into the game. Let us first ask if it is possible to use a computer to interpret a horoscope. We must make a distinction between calculating the stellar configurations for the time of birth, which is an astronomical operation, and interpreting them, which is an astrological one.

Theoretically, there is no great difficulty in establishing a computer program that permits us to obtain the position of the planets in the horoscope for the place and moment of birth. It is enough to consult the ephemeris in which the astronomers have published their calculations. The program is thus established and placed into the memory banks of the machine. And this will furnish the positions of the planets for every birthdate in the two given periods of time (1880 to 1980 for example).

The difficulty begins when it becomes necessary to program the interpretation of the horoscope. Let us put ourselves in the astrologer's place and with him, ask how he must proceed. The components of a complete classic horoscope are known. There is first of all the position of the sun, moon and the eight planets in the twelve signs of the zodiac on the day of birth. Then there is their position in one of the twelve houses, which depends on the hour of birth; and finally the good and bad aspects formed between the planets. But we must also consider the ascendant; and still many other things. . . .

A horoscope is a highly complex entity. This is why there are not two identical horoscopes, except for an identical time and place of birth. Its interpretation is very delicate work, we are told, and demands a great deal of knowledge and intuition on the part of the astrologer. All of these interpretive factors would have to be placed in the memory bank of the computer. But there are technical and, above all, financial limitations (after all, this is a solely commercial undertaking) that can oblige the astrologer to considerably simplify his formulas. No doubt he will write interpretive sketches for a limited number of astral configurations and these, making up the program, will be punched on IBM cards. When the moment has come, the computer, thanks to a teleprinter, will neatly type out an interpretation for the client. It will be docily printed, but it might be feared that such an interpretation will lack an over-all synthesis of the factor involved.

This is why we are skeptical when it is asserted that "Ordinamus is much more than a horoscope." On the contrary, one must think that the horoscope's journey through the innards of a computer gives us much less than a horoscope: the skeleton of a horoscope, or more precisely, the disconnected parts of the skeleton. Once these reservations are made, nothing opposes using the computer to do mass-produced horoscopes. We will go even further: if there is anything true in astrology, a synthesis that might appear too approximative to the purist seems here to be a *positive element.* The experiment will better reveal the elementary constants that are favorable to astrology. This is of course if the horoscopic program harbors any. For let us not forget that computers are "dumb," and if an astrologer's program is an absurdity, the machine will do no more than regurgitate this absurdity. Our investigation revolves precisely around this point.

Our study begins in a very banal way. Like every potential purchaser of an electronic horoscope, we wrote to *Ordinamus* for information; the advertisements had suggested emphatically that we do precisely that. We received an imposing reply, lavishly illustrated and temptingly worded to help us come to terms with the cost of the service:

Dear Sir:
How right you are! Here is the information you requested. You will quickly understand that the scientific astrology of Ordinamus can bring you astonishing revelations. The use of this tireless and precise computer has permitted us to bring the consultation fee down from 500 Francs ($110) (the average fee of a great astrologer) to 120 Francs ($30) . . . . And this dossier will be your companion, a precious friend that you will consult throughout the coming ten years; for an Ordinamus study tells you in clearest terms all the future events—whether happy or difficult—that you can reasonably expect for the next ten years. . . . Perhaps you will soon be entering a lucky period! Don't wait a moment to find out. Send us your order form today!

How could we resist? One, two or even three cases however, are not sufficient to permit a conclusion on the validity of these alleged predictions. With *Science et Vie,* we decided to perform the study on ten horoscopes. There remained the problem of choosing the birthdates. For this, we had to devise an honest control, that is to say, we had to ask of Ordinamus no more than the astrologer declares himself capable of doing. Now, what exactly was offered for 120 Francs? Summing up:

1. the full chart of your astral heavens;
2. your psychological portrait: an "in depth" analysis of your personality;
3. the annual calendar of your life rhythm;
4. the lucky and unlucky periods of your life for the next ten years.

In other words, the emphasis was on character and destiny. We therefore had to choose individuals whose character traits were salient—even extreme—and whose destiny were equally remarkable. The horoscopes of contemporary personalities (DeGaulle, Lyndon Johnson, Mao, etc.) were cautiously eliminated: every astrologer worthy of the name knows these birthdates by heart.[3] We made our choice from among individuals at the other end of the scale: convicted criminals. Ten criminals that offered extreme character traits and a catastrophic life pattern were gathered to serve as the astrological material in our test.

In our opinion it was an excellent test. But it also had to meet the approval of the astrologer. We were reassured on this point. In one of his twenty-six books, he states that criminal tendencies can be read in a horoscope. For him it is the planet Mars that creates murderers, "those who are butchers." And he adds the following statement: "The following equation can be presented: Mars = murderers, butchers, soldiers, doctors = oral sadistic stage . . . I have found a very clear Mars-Saturn dominant in the 'stars of crime.' "[4]

Our experiment could thus be a good occasion for astrologers to verify their astro-psychoanalytical theories. But if, by chance, they were not able to discover the essential of the personalities and destinies of the criminals in our test, how could they hope to do so for average men and women? It would be difficult for astrology to survive such a blow. The experiment promised to be crucial.

Finally, let us make it clear, that we had no intention of fooling the astrologer, and that the ten criminals were indeed the only ones about of whom we asked *Ordinamus* to do a horoscope.

Our sources—as far as they involve the thoughts and acts of the individuals and the penalties which they eventually suffered—were carefully chosen. They will be cited and in case of disagreement, the astrologer can easily refer to them. On our part, we are carefully keeping the ten dossiers in our files, the dossiers which, for 120 Francs a piece, became our property.

One last technical point: we had to know as exactly as possible the place, date and hour of birth of the subjects of our experimental group. We consequently followed the advice of *Ordinamus*: "The hour of birth, a most important piece of information, can be obtained from the civil registry of the place of birth." We thus wrote and received birth certificates with the hour of birth. All of these replies bear the seal of appropriate authorities and have been preserved as proof.

There was nothing left to do but send in the ten coupons for the horoscopes to Ordinamus. In order to not give ourselves away however, we gave borrowed names and addresses. In a reasonable time, we had in our possession the ten horoscopes from the programming of "the leader of modern astrology." Ten pieces of evidence, and we shall shortly examine their dossiers, including, of course, the biographical references for each one.[5]

The criminals' horoscope

Each Ordinamus provided two kinds of documents. An astronomical document and an astrological document. The first was the chart of the heavens, drawn by an electronic plotter and accompanied by a list of planetary positions to the nearest degree in "Signs," and "Houses," and the "Notable Aspects." We checked these figures with the help of astronomical tables *(Annuaire du bureau des Longitudes, Connaissance des Temps)*. The impression was rather favorable: within a margin of two degrees the planetary positions provided by Ordinamus did not differ from those calculated by astronomers. It is true that here the astrologer has only to copy the astronomer's work: but he seems to have done it correctly.

There remains the essential part of what we are after: the astrological prediction. Glancing through the ten Ordinamus files we noted a fairly decent variation from one interpretation of one horoscope to another, apparently an attempt to "personalize" them. It was not complete, however. Three of the horoscopes begin with the same paragraph, and in the "psychological profile" alone, we find five paragraphs which are duplicated throughout the ten natal charts. Also, there are several cases of two paragraphs, one following immediately upon the other, which deal with the same topic but unequivocally contradict one another. For example, in horoscope #3, in the section on "Romantic Destiny" it states:

Disposition to happy love, one that is warm, gay, generous or full. It is love that is experienced in fresh and healthy *joie de vivre* . . .

There follows on the very next line:

Tendency toward a fragmented love life; tenderness and physical attraction do not go hand to hand. Love must be experienced as a struggle, on the battlefield, as it were . . .

There is no doubt that we are in the presence of two mutually exclusive astrological elements which the machine was unable to synthesize. The program is short, much too short.[6]

But each astrological translation was justified by an astronomical configuration and, as we have already pointed out, if there is anything true in astrology, even an exaggerated synthesis could only make criminal tendencies of the individual in question more explicit. The astrologer followed the guiding thread of traditional astrology. We were not dealing with someone ignorant of the royal art of the heavenly bodies—far from it. As such, the experiment undertaken could only have more bearing and the conclusions drawn on the validity of the horoscope in general could only have more weight.

In order to establish a complete comparison between each horoscope and reality, we constructed a case-book for each criminal. These case-books were divided in two vertically. On the right, we transcribed the astrological interpretation: on the left, those things which actually happened. In all, an imposing collection of documents, weighing four and a half pounds and measuring eight inches high, was constituted. Reproducing them here is out of the question: for the transcription of the Ordinamus files alone, fifty pages of this book would be necessary. However, we have reproduced the shortest "psychological profile" that we received (see p. 116: Brice). Let us now go over each case in numerical order. The complete documentation on each case is of course open to the perusal of astrologers, in case they wish to lodge a protest.

Dr. Marcel Petiot

Born in Auxerre (Yonne) on January 17, 1897, at 3 A.M. Arrested on October 31, 1944, and accused of 27 murders. Sentenced to death and executed on May 26, 1946 (c.f. Marcel Montaron, *Les Grandes proces d'Assises,* C.A.L. Ch. 9, "Petiot le diabolique," pp. 165–85).

One of a kind, the "satanic" Dr. Petiot was "one of the greatest criminals in the annals of penal law," according to Montaron, to whom we owe the following biographical information. His trial in 1946 aroused enormous interest. The accused, a physician of dubious merit who had previously led a hectic existence, one day struck upon the profitable idea of undertaking a criminal scenario. It was during the Second World War and France was under occupation. Petiot was in touch with people who were trying to escape the persecution of the Nazis, and he made them believe that he could get them out of France to South America, where they could live in safety. On an appointed day, the unfortunate people arrived at Petiot's home, in the rue le Sueur in Paris, with their money and their most treasured belongings. Petiot murdered them and dissolved their bodies in a tub of quicklime that had been built in a secret chamber. The indictment only charged the doctor with 27 murders, but the number was probably much greater. Petiot himself, who never lost his insolence or boastfulness during the trial, declared that he had murdered 63 people.

Let us now open the Ordinamus of Dr. Petiot, and examine first of all what his "psychological profile" says. It begins with a description of the subject "in the framework of his social world.":

As he is a Virgo, Jovian, instinctive warmth or power is allied with the resources of the intellect, lucidity, wit. His adaptable and pliant character expresses itself through skill and efficiency; his dynamism finds support in a tendency towards order, control, balance. He is an organized and organizing person socially, materially, or intellectually. He may appear as someone who submits himself to social norms, fond of propriety, and endowed with a moral sense which is comforting—that of a worthy, right-thinking, middle-class citizen.

After the social environment, Ordinamus describes the subject "as he is in his true self."

As a Uranus-Saturn type . . . he tends to build for himself a universe which is selective and personal . . . in which rigor, discipline, severity, austerity or asceticism may reign.

Finally, the astrologer describes Petiot "at home, in the framework of his private universe, within his inner being." The portrait becomes more and more surprising and seems touched with patches of black humor to anyone who knows who the subject really is:

> This Venusian being is bathed in an ocean of sensitivity diffusing out to the infinite and crossed currents of love for mankind . . . [but his victim suffered from diffusion in a very different medium] . . . sentiments which are more or less tinged by the romantic, the strange, the ethereal or the mystical, but which usually find their expression in total devotion to others, redeeming love, or altruistic sacrifices. . . . a tendency to be more pleasant in one's own home, to love one's house, to enjoy having a charming home . . . [furnished, as we have seen, with the most charming conveniences].

Arrested in October, 1944, Petiot was tried in March, 1946, and was condemned to death. What does his horoscope say about this period of the year? Let us consult the chapter in Ordinamus on "annual rhythm," a chart, we are told, that "indicates a regular rhythm that returns each year in the form of periods of one or two weeks when your various potentialities are aroused." Consulting this convenient little table for the date when Petiot was arrested, we find a time during which nothing should have happened. In March, on the other hand, when Petiot was condemned to death, the period corresponds to "Venusian Undertone" (from February 26 to March 11, to be exact):

> The subject tends to belong wholeheartedly to his Venusian nature, and his feelings, familial ties, his home, and his intimate inner life are in the forefront [one might say that a clamorous trial is somewhat removed from an intimate inner life.]

But the crowning glory of Ordinamus is the astral calendar, the prediction for ten years beginning in 1968. Since Petiot was executed in 1946, what meaning can his astral calendar for 1968–78 possibly have? Well, a great deal: between these two dates, many ups and downs of Petiot's life are indicated. Between the end of 1970 and the middle of 1972, for example, Petiot was supposed to have "a tendency to make commitments regarding his romantic life . . ."[7]

The priest of Uruffe

Father Guy Desnoyers, priest of Uruffe, born on February 24, 1920, 8 A.M. in Gerbecourt-et-Happlemont, Meurthe et Moselle, murdered a young girl who was his mistress. In January, 1958, he was sentenced to life imprisonment at hard labor (Montaron, *op.cit.*, Ch. 12, pp. 221–237).

Desnoyers' trial in 1956 aroused much public indignation, for "this priest, who had had relations with a young girl in the village, shot her through the neck when he discovered that she was pregnant with his child. Then, in order to erase every trace of this unwanted paternity, he disemboweled the unfortunate girl and disfigured the fetus." (*Ibid.*, p. 221.)

Here is how Ordinamus opens the subject of Desnoyers. The client is being described "within the framework of his career":

> This Saturnian applies a constant restraint to his instinctive drives . . . , his character is timorous and timid . . . and subject to excessive scruples. Prudent, orderly and serious, . . . a nervous person who can find a guiding light for his mind and has a chance to realize himself through intellectualization. . . .[8]

This portrait of the priest is diametrically opposed to the truth. According to Montaron "From the very beginning he was considered in the village as a dynamic, modern pastor, but devoid of any intellectual aspirations. . . . For the young people in the village, he tried to increase the opportunities for recreation. One summer, there had been mixed swimming on the Cote d'Azur beach, girls and priest all in bathing suits for what Desnoyers liked about the ecclesiastic calling was not the meditative life or sermons composed in a profound faith, but rather the life in the world" (*Ibid.*, pp. 228–9).

Once before, the astonishing priest had relations with a young girl, and the scandal was about to break loose in the village. But taken in hand by Desnoyers, the girl left to abandon the fruit of her sin to the South of France. As Montaron remarks "Perhaps the scandal would have been better," for it might have prevented the priest of Uruffe from committing his double murder.

It can unfortunately in no way be said that Desnoyers, "in the framework of his career," "applies a constant restraint to his instinctive drives." Further on his "psychological profile," he is described as a "kind and humane" person: there is question of his "gift of himself, his achieving sacrifice." We can put an end to these references. His crime was committed at the beginning of December, 1956. No matter how hard one looks, one finds nothing for this period of the year in his horoscope. He was tried and sentenced to hard labor for life in January, 1958. For this date Ordinamus tells us:

Venusian undertones . . . During this Venusian week, the subject is open to the many manifestations of love, sympathy or favor from others.

As for the good and bad predictions for the ten subsequent years, what significance can they have for a prisoner leading the drab existence of a "lifer" in a tiny cell of the Saint Malo penitentiary?

Albert Millet

"The Killer of Hyeres," this gangster guilty of two murders, born in Hyeres (Var) on July 2, 1929, at 5 P.M., was sentenced at hard labor for life (see *France-Soir,* April 5, 1954).

France-Soir said of him: "Born in Hyeres, Millet is a frightening hoodlum. With a gang of accomplices, he terrorized the city for several years. At the age of fifteen, he had been sent to Juvenile Court, and at seventeen, he was sent to prison. Upon his release, he organized a gang that specialized in the burglary of country homes. Returning from military service, he became known when, caught in the act of robbery by a policeman, he shot at the officer (without hitting him). Following a recent settling of accounts, Millet attacked a North African who, although his lung was perforated by a bullet, miraculously escaped death. In a night club he noticed a fifteen year old servant girl, Paulette D., and decided to have her work for him. The girl informed her family and her aunt threatened to call the police if he did not leave her niece alone. Millet then decided to arrange things. "In the center of Hyeres, he came up to his victim, calmly put a pistol to her chest, shot her, and fled." Arrested a short time later, Millet was sentenced to life at hard labor.

And here is the "psychological profile" given by the astrologer for "The Killer of Hyeres":

A happy, euphoric nature . . . The climate of his life is springlike, sunny, happily elegant and worldly if not comfortably well-off. His gay, agreeable, and warm character, full of liveliness and communicative good humor, is made for happiness . . . It is easy to imagine this chatty and travelling being having a joking humor [!] . . . , he bends willingly, is conciliating and cooperative [!], . . . Tends to lead a joyful love-life, warm, generous, and full. A love which expresses itself in a frank and healthy *joie de vivre.* . .

Since the rest is in the same vein, let us not delay in moving to the next case.

Mrs. Ducourneau

Elisabeth Lamouly, the wife of a certain Ducourneau, was born on September 1, 1904, 6 A.M. in Belin (Gironde). She poisoned her mother and husband, was sentenced to death and executed on January 8, 1941 (Judicial Archives).

Elisabeth Ducourneau was the last woman to be executed in France. It happened during the occupation. She had poisoned her mother and husband who—as she put it—"got in the way of her future plans." An anecdote related by Montaron gives us an idea of the cultural and intellectual level of this criminal. On the morning of her execution, "the condemned woman did not at first understand the picturesque but customary formula used by the director of the penitentiary when she was to be taken from her cell: 'the time has come to pay your debt to society,' she believed that she had to pay the costs of her trial. 'But I have some money,' she exclaimed. It was the guardian of the woman's section who explained to her what was happening" (*op. cit.*, p. 127).

Let us now hear what Ordinamus has to say:

> The Virgo basis of this personality tends to suppress the influence of instinct and to impose the values of the intellect. . . . Here we have the creature of reason . . . who fashions for herself a moral world made up of reserve, sobriety, economy, discipline, mastery, scrupulousness, respectability, purity, and perfection.

On the other hand, Ordinamus is totally silent about the day of her execution (January 8, 1941). It recalls to mind that on the day of the fall of the Bastille, the day that marks the beginning of the French Revolution, King Louis XVI wrote in his diary "Nothing today."

Simone Macrides

Simone Macrides was born on January 23, 1924, 5 A.M., in Croix (Nord). On February 28, 1966, she kidnapped a newborn child and tried to pass it off as her own (*Detective:* 1028).

Her case is somewhat different than the preceding ones, for she was not a murderer. It was rather an exacerbated maternal love that brought her before the law. Haunted by the desire to have a daughter of her own, she played an incredible drama for her credulous husband. Claiming to be pregnant, she went to have the baby far from her home. On February 28, 1966, she kidnapped a newborn girl and took it to her home. But this criminal deception was rapidly discovered. Here is the beginning of her astrological portrait, signed by the astrologer:

> The double planetary signature of Jupiter and Saturn situate her in the line of a personality gifted with psychological maturity and a strong, solid, and stable character . . . , This is a deep person, unshakable, self-possessed, a classical character who inspires respect. Her strength rests on order, discipline, reflection, and judgment. . . . In her are united the bourgeois, the clerk, the notary and possibly the sage. . . .

Need we go on? The following prediction is found in Ordinamus for February 28, the day when Simone Macrides committed her crime:

> Venusian undertone from February 19 to March 4 . . . in general life tends to be easy, with *joie de vivre* and happiness.

Andre Martin

Andre Joseph Martin, born in Trouhans (Côte-d'Or) on March 19, 1912, at 7 A.M., killed his wife on March 8, 1940, in a fit of jealousy (Prof. Lagache, *La Jalousie amoureuse,* Vol. II., pp. 257–286).

In his *La Jalousie amoureuse,* Prof. Lagache has given a profound analysis of this case. In his opinion in fact, Martin was above all a jealous man "who thought of the murder as an act of justice. After the crime, Martin sought to legitimize his act, qualifying it as a reaction of defense and anger; he acted like a victim; and there was a constant railing against his rivals, against the judges, and so on. Characterologically, Martin was a delinquent."[9] If not quite so clear, Ordinamus is more lyrical:

> The subject presents himself as a Neptunian type. The basic disposition of his personality is one of great psychic plasticity, which expresses itself as receptivity, osmosis, availability, and an infinite and indefinite psychic malleability: For him, the social environment plays a role similar to that of the ocean for the fish. . . .

This is all nonsense. Let us go a little further:

> ... this interior being inclines the ego to spread itself out, to diffuse, to dilute itself in its surroundings, so as to find an infinite echo for itself. ...

Not much better: let us proceed to the end of the paragraph:

> It is a sweet and good nature.

At last we understand!

Pierre Fouesnant

Born in Landaul (Morbihan) on May 21, 1943, at 10 A.M., Pierre Fouesnant killed his unfaithful mistress. (*Detective:* 1130)

It was in fact a rather banal murder. Fouesnant abandoned his wife for a more chic and expert mistress. She was not content with one lover however, and deceived him openly. Fouesnant did not accept this sharing and killed his mistress with a knife. His astrological portrait begins like this:

> This Venusian being, colored by lunar values, is an emotional type, susceptible to palpitations of the soul. This most often makes one sentimental, wrapped up in the inner life ..., one of tenderness, goodness, sweetness, charm, and grace. He aspires to a calm and deep happiness ... completed with delightful and delicate intimacy, where the love of home and hearth dominate ... [later on] good sense ... good father ...

Let us note that the day of the crime—February 12, 1968—nothing important happens according to his horoscope.

Jacques Marie

Jacques Marie was born in Vassy (Calvadoes) on May 15, 1926, 4 P.M., and on March 2, 1966, killed his wife for reasons that are not clear (*Detective:* 1028).

"He was certainly not very happy," writes *Detective,* where we find the story of this case. A depressed and nervous farmer, Marie killed his wife for rather obscure reasons and immediately committed suicide. The astrologer nonetheless predicted a future for him until 1978, and describes thus the murderer "within the framework of his marital union":

> This Venusian nature expresses itself in a lively, playful, and spontaneous way, a captivating personality, expansive gaiety and alluring zest. . . . Venus presides over the fate of marriage. This constitutes a fortunate indication for the sentimental side of life. . . . His marriage has a great possibility of being harmonious and happy. . . .

Conclude the ceremony!

Ralph Kuhn

A hoodlum condemned to hard labor, Ralph Kuhn was born on March 3, 1944, in Amnéville (Moselle) at 5:25 A.M. (*Detective:* 998).

It is said that this young thug "dreamed of being an intellectual of crime," and on May 19, 1965, he murdered a delivery man during a holdup. He was arrested a short time later and sentenced to prison. His birthdate did not greatly inspire Ordinamus:

> The subject has a personal psychological makeup which is very difficult to unravel!

Even so, we are told later:

> that there is a disposition to love stability, the love of peaceful and calm feelings, feelings that are simple, honest, faithful, and durable. . . .

But we read on the following line:

> an indication of a broken engagement or sentimental irregularities that can result in a penchant for pleasure, easy living, and enjoyment.

Obviously, the astrologer is completely lost here as well.

Alfred Brice

Alfred Brice was born in Haubourdin (Nord) on January 27, 1928, at 5:00 P.M., and killed his wife on February 16, 1966 (*Detective:* 1026).

We will extensively reproduce this case in order to show how the results of the experiment were analyzed. Brice's "psychological" Ordinamus is given word for word, side by side with the real behavior of the murderer.

What Ordinamus says	*What really happened*
It is in the universe of work that the subject tends to give the essential of himself. There he can reveal himself, realize himself and bloom. Moreover, he tends to exert a natural authority over those who are his subordinates: employees, servants. . . . There is a tendency to grow by travelling, to find his true dimensions through interchange with foreigners or going abroad: such is the environment where he is most propitious to find deep satisfaction or success.	An occasional handy-man, Brice never stayed on one job more than two or three weeks; evidently the couple had financial difficulties. Family harmony suffered from this, as did the children's education.
The subject fashions his success with his own qualities: a powerful personality, a magnetic charm, social brilliance, and know-how, the ability to make up his own mind, professional aptitudes.	
Through his solar nature, the subject belongs to the Aquarius type. He is a being with a refined, airy essence who tends to strip himself of his instincts, to be free of the domination of his passions, preferring a spiritual state. In him there is an "angelic" sensitivity, a delicate, limpid, enlightened, and ethereal soul which lives in the joy of altruistic self-abandonment— whether it be expressed as hos-	No one would have guessed that Brice had incestuous designs toward the half-sister of his children. When Claudine began to turn into a young woman before his eyes, there perhaps occurred in the mind of the head of the family what psychoanalysis calls "transfer." The privilege of being first, of which he had been deprived by Mrs. Brice, he now felt irresistibly that he could extract from the daughter.

pitable warmth, advice, helpful-
ness, or friendship. An idealism
who sometimes gets lost in his
dream-world. But this sensitivity can be muzzled by repressive
factors, in which case it is replaced by pure intellectuality.
The subject then appears as a
clear-minded, lucid being, made
independent by his ideas, free in
his manner, modern in his expression, original, if not eccentric or maladapted. His dynamism can cause him to like the
avant-garde, anticipations, risk,
and adventure.

As a Mercurian type he is
basically nervous, one whose
strength tends to be situated in a
dynamic mind. His personal development grows along with a
certain originality, if not through
a certain idealistic generosity.

The subject often has a hunger for adventure, and this may
make him uncomfortable in his
surroundings. He is on the look-
out for anything which might
emancipate him, remove his
ties, reveal new horizons. Re-
sourceful and intuitive, he is
able to anticipate developments,
assimilate ideas ahead of their
time, and pave the way for the
future. He is modern, progres-
sive, reform-minded, revolutionary, or simply utopian, chimeric,
and adventurous. He may have a
remarkable life if he chooses to
dedicate himself to a humane
cause, to serve an ideal, to become the spokesman of wisdom,

His acts became suspect, and
were soon to alarm his wife. . . .
Then his desires became demanding; he no longer cared
whether or not his wife was present. One day he locked his wife
in the cellar and went after the
attractive little Claudine, who
just barely escaped. Brice, who
had always been a sober man,
began to drink. On February
16, . . . he drank a whole bottle
of champagne alone and soon
lost control.

Exasperated by his wife's
begging, he struck her with a
garden tool, and she fell dead to
the ground. . . .

(When Claudine returned
from school) . . . the criminal
husband dragged away this frail
blond little girl who had aroused
in him both a bestial desire and
a keen thirst for revenge.
(*Detective:* 1026, February 24,
1966, p. 29).

to magnify friendship, to be a
psychological counselor, or to become more intellectual, or more
spiritual.

In none of the ten Ordinamus just examined did we find a prediction of the criminal dispositions or fate of the subjects of our
sample. But there is a defect which is even more serious for astrology. For the failure to predict a criminal future might be excused,
provided that the *subject's general character* was adequately
sketched. But none of the astrological portraits bore any resemblance to the real-life model.

Petiot's cynicism, the sexual problems of Brice and the priest of
Uruffe, Millet's aggressiveness, Marie's murderous anguish, and so
on: none of this is found in their horoscopes. The frustrated and
exacerbated maternal love of Simone Macrides is not mentioned
either. Petiot and Millet are described as "middle-class," the priest,
Brice, and Mrs. Ducourneau as "intellectuals," and Simone Macrides as "well-balanced." As for the predictions, (the annual rhythm
for ten years)—inasmuch as the astrologer truly applied an astrological program—they in no way reflect the reality of the subjects'
situations.

Even when it is programmed by a renowned astrologer, the
horoscope cannot seize the main features of an individual's fate.
Such a total humiliating and conclusive defeat is quite surprising.
The astrologer's interpretations are diametrically opposed to the
truth—they are not merely "chance replies." There is an explanation to this phenomenon. The astrologer's interpretations have been
wisely prepared in order to satisfy ordinary people who are always
ready to accept as gospel truth any pretentious, vague, cloudy, and
pseudopsychological jargon, as long as they are the subject thereof.
For like its ancestor written on parchment, the computerized horoscope creates illusion. The client is satisfied with the doubtful product that he has purchased. And here we find the leitmotif of astrology: the clientele is satisfied, therefore the horoscope is true. For its
part, Ordinamus speaks of "thousands of enthusiastic testimonials"
like: "It was fantastic to recognize myself in the portrait. . . ." The
astrologer states that eight out of ten people are completely satisfied with the horoscope. Is it just boasting? Hardly. Experiments by
professional psychologists permit us to assume that this is very
probable.

Astrological testimony

From a random sample of individuals, a great majority believe that they recognize themselves in character analyses presented to them, even if the analysis does not concern them in any way. Richard Meili, a professor at the Rousseau Institute in Geneva, has published in the *Archives de Psychologie* the results of a poll that might be surprising to those unfamiliar with the psychology of everyday life. Twenty-five hundred judgments of character were given *at random* to a few hundred subjects. This did not prevent these subjects from considering that these judgments described their personality with a surprising accuracy. It is true that these subjects were not informed of the role of chance in this experiment. Professor Meili concludes that "fictive diagnoses applied at random will satisfy the public to a large degree if one remains rather vague and prudent in the judgments presented."[10]

And when it is known that the subject of Meili's experiments were students in psychology, one begins to get an idea of the unfathomable depths where testimony sends us. It might have been thought that this group would be more able to judge the reality of such an all-purpose portrait.

As for objectivity, it goes without saying that astrological testimony could not be superior to others. Moreover, the fact of investing to the tune of 120 Francs in a horoscope is the sign of a certain credulity. Whatever their cultural level, the clients represent a group that are, one might say, "in a state of lesser astrological resistance." How can these clients struggle against the astrologer's wile and against his cloudy but flattering jargon, where each paragraph is a model of *"yes, but . . . ,"* where the thesis is always followed by the antithesis, but where the synthesis is always lacking? It is difficult to demonstrate enough critical sense to oppose 2,000 years of astrological *savoir-faire*. This is what the crafty, if not knowledgeable, astrologer hopes.

Ordinamus, for example, does not fail to include a questionnaire called "control card" that asks the customer: "Did you recognize yourself in the personality profile?" Positive answers are elicited by flattering the client, by holding out the prospect of a (free?) "follow-up" to his horoscope: "If you so desire, this document can help you in a further expansion of your horoscope at a later date." This is the source of the "satisfied customers" included in their advertising brochures. They permit an increase in the number of clients. It is perhaps even more serious: it is claimed that these testimonials are a proof of the validity of the horoscopes, and are examined by a "committee composed of scientists, both in favor of and opposed to astrology." This attempt at astrological infiltration will not surprise the true man of science, but it is good to give the astrologer a fairer sense of proportions.

Dr. Louis Couderc, formerly of the Seine Psychiatric Hospital, devoted himself "for some time to the astrological profession" and was dumbfounded by his success and praise. He began by publishing an advertisement and was submerged by responses from all quarters. He sent the same letter to each correspondent and received a voluminous response: he had more than two hundred answers, filled with sentences like: "What you say of my past and my character is the absolute truth"; or "I can say that you read my life like a book."[11] But Dr. Couderc's experiment took place in 1937. Perhaps the previous generation was more credulous than we. Thus, rather than inventing a universal letter, it seemed preferable to take account of the effect on the clientele of the astrologer's jargon today. Thus we decided to play the part of the fakir, and, with the collaboration of the magazine *Science et Vie,* we created *Astral Electronics.*

Astral Electronics

Here is the advertisement that we published (in *Ici-Paris,* April 16, 1968):[12]

ABSOLUTELY FREE
YOUR ULTRA-PERSONAL HOROSCOPE

a 10 page document

Don't miss this unique opportunity
Send your name, address, date and
place of birth to:
ASTRAL ELECTRONICS
8 Rue Amyot
Paris 5

Compared to the large billboards of Ordinamus and the others, our little ad seemed no more than David facing Goliath. Nonetheless, shortly after its publication, our mail box was stuffed with letters and continued to be *filled* for several weeks. Requests for ULTRA-PERSONAL HOROSCOPES came from all parts of France, and even from abroad (one came from Reunion Island and another from Guadaloupe). Ten years later, we are still receiving requests! The reader will no doubt be interested in some statistics: 70 percent women and 30 percent men; an average age of thirty-five years; and 65 percent were from outside the Parisian region. Several people declared that they were in difficulty, having problems with their health, money, or their personal life. Our small sample is probably just about similar to an astrologer's clientele, although perhaps a little less fortunate or a little less devoted to astrology (for remember that, needless to say, we bear all the cost of the experiment. Our answers were *really* absolutely free).

To each one of our 150-odd correspondents we sent *the same horoscope*. But not just any horoscope. We sent one of those we had received from Ordinamus; to be precise, that of the most infamous evildoer in our collection, Dr. Petiot. We reproduced the psychological profile and the yearly rhythm of this horoscope *without changing so much as a comma*. Along with it we enclosed a reply form similar to the one which came from Ordinamus: we asked our correspondents to tell us if they recognized themselves easily in the free horoscope we had given them. A stamped, self-addressed envelope was the final piece in our package.

A few days later we were able to read dozens of completely positive responses. We were even being offered money for more detailed analyses. We already had the beginnings of a small clientele tied hand and foot to our will.

To our first question—"Did you recognize yourself in the psychological portrait sent you? Did you recognize any of your personal problems?"—we received a positive answer in 94 percent of the replies.

The second question—"Is your opinion shared by your family and friends?"—brought a 90 percent positive reply.

The third question—"Does the annual rhythm generally indicate the good and bad periods you experience each year?"—brought an 80 percent positive reply as well.

Here are a few testimonials taken from our mail that we have retained for evidence in case of eventual need:

Question 1.

The work done by this machine is marvelous . . . I would go so far as to say extraordinary. I have underlined passages in the horoscope which certainly are applicable to me and which are true. It is a pleasure to send them to you. (Mrs. H. M. Draveil.)

It is certainly me, and I can now understand certain contradictions in my character. Can astrology find solutions for them? (Mr. A. D. Paris.)

I easily recognized myself in this psychological portrait, and they are precisely my own personal problems. (Mrs. J. R., Lorient.)

Yes, I recognized my personal problems. It is absolutely bewildering that an electronic machine is able to probe people's character and future. (Mr. R. A., Douarnenez.)

Question 2.

On the whole, everyone who knows me found it accurate, and especially my wife, who knows me perfectly well. (Mr. D. A., Paris.)

Yes, I recognized my personal problems. This opinion is shared by my family and friends. (Mrs. R. E. E., Montpelier.)

I showed the horoscope to my parents and to a friend, and they were astonished by its accuracy. (Mrs. J. R., Lorient.)

Undeniably yes, says my wife. (Mr. R. H., Le Fresnay/Sarthe.)

Question 3.

Yes, especially from 1/22 to 2/7 (desire for long trips, change of climate). During this period I applied for permission to emigrate to Australia. (Mr. A. B., Besancon.)

Yes, for November, since I was ill (severe rheumatism). In August, I made arrangements and was married in October. (Mr. J. G., Le Vesinet.)

One can see that in the ten-page horoscope, each person falls upon the passage that strikes him with its accuracy. Events predicted in Petiot's horoscope did indeed occur . . . for other individuals. As Saint Augustine noted in his *Confessions,* chance is a great psychologist:

For is when a man by chance opens the pages of some poet, who sang and thought of something wholly different, a verse often-times fell out, wondrously agreeable to the present business: it were not to be wondered at, if out of the soul of man, unconscious what takes place in it, by some higher instinct an answer should be given, by hap, not by art, corresponding to the business and actions of the demander.[13]

This is why nearly all of our "clients"—nine out of ten—recognized themselves in the horoscope of someone who murdered several dozens of people and then dissolved their bodies in lime. It is thus not at all incorrect for the astrologer to say that he is "successful" eight times out of ten. We hope at least that the "leader of modern astrology" will not be upset that we beat his own record, since he is still responsible. He has so stacked the deck with his "yes, no, even so" style that the trick "works" almost every time. The unfortunate thing is that it did not work at all in the case of the one and only authentic bearer of the horoscope: Dr. Petiot. Though the public can always be bamboozled by the "computer tamers," it is finally the astrologer who is devoured by the electronic ogre when his merchandise is examined with objectivity. An unfortunate boomerang.

The cautious astrologer

Our experiment on human testimony will have shown at least that intelligent men and women listen respectfully to the expensive vaticinations of astrologers. But the astrologer-programmer of Ordinamus ought not to be afraid that our scientific experiment will cause him to lose any clients: the hen that lays golden eggs cannot be killed by anyone who so wishes. And then, the practitioner will not be short on excuses. For he is very cautious.

Surprisingly, opposed to the pompous and imprudent statements of Ordinamus' advertisements, the client notes that the tone changes once his request has been recorded. Caution now reigns. The Ordinamus horoscope is accompanied by numerous warnings like:

The validity of this study—and especially the first part of the psychological profile—would be questionable if the hour of birth . . . were not completely exact. . . . With a ten-minute, or even a four-minute difference from the exact moment, the basic lines of the sketch begin to change and can even be completely revised in the case of a birth artificially provoked or determined primarily by medical intervention.

When one realizes that it is almost impossible to know the moment of birth within five minutes, and that nowadays the practice of "induced" childbirth is widespread, one understands that the astrologer carefully prepares exits in case of failure. It is a shame however, that this caution becomes apparent *after* the client has paid, and that the astrologer has not bothered to make his points in the abundant documentation sent before hand.[14]

In the end, is the astrologer really "ethical"? So far we have not asked ourselves this question, having preferred simply to examine the facts with impartiality and to judge the evidence. But numerous indications that have turned up throughout the study give a bad impression.

Is it ethical to cast someone's horoscope without taking sex, socio-economic class, or the level of education in account? Ordinamus treats the problems of a twenty-year-old country girl in the same standardized way as those of a seventy-year-old top executive. Neither has the weight of heredity on an individual's destiny been taken into account. The astrologer does not even estimate that it might interfere with astral influence. But certain scientific studies have led to the supposition that some criminal predispositions might come from chromosomal aberration. This had already been the subject of court cases in France. The case of the murderer Daniel Hugon was remanded once before being tried, for his attorney established that his client had one Y chromosome too many. We can also note that Richard Speck, who brutally murdered eight student nurses in Chicago in 1966, had an extra chromosome as well. But in the eyes of the astrologers, would hereditary factors be less important in an individual's destiny than the position of Neptune on the day of birth?

It is true that the only goal of computerized astrology is sales. A final anecdote will confirm this. Our study was almost over when our attention was drawn to a new brand of computerized horoscope advertised in the press: Electrostar:[15]

Exceptional offer: only 20 Francs
Your personalized horoscope.
A seven page document . . . astonishing revelations . . .
unbelievable but true . . . L. C. H., the great astrologer, etc.

You might think that this would be a more moderately priced competitor of Ordinamus. It is nothing of the kind. The address of Electrostar is THE SAME as that of Ordinamus, and L. C. H. has no existence of his own, being the (astral) double of B., the author of twenty-six books, the "leader of modern astrology." From a letter sent by Ordinamus we understood that Electrostar is nothing but bait for the 120-Franc trap of Ordinamus. We were curious, and sent for this bargain-basement horoscope for the birth of Dr. Petiot. Even though it was programmed "under the supervision" of the same astrologer, it contained a totally different psychological interpretation: it could not have been otherwise: the brand-name horoscopic program is not the same as the off-brand. Space does not permit a detailed comparison, although it would be instructive. But from this little story the reader can appreciate the seriousness of computerized astrology without our expanding on it. It illuminates the sales mechanisms of today's astrological product.

In essence, the method has scarcely evolved since the famous Fakir Birman and finally, it is a little saddening to find charlatans operating the computers. Astrology's "Copernican revolution" has turned into a gadget. For several years, Electrostar has been sold in Paris on the famous Champs Elysées Avenue in a luxurious little shop decorated in gold. Several color television sets at the door go full blast to attract passers-by and entice them in. Their sonorous images have replaced the barker of old. But let us lower the curtain, for the astrologer must be tired, and so are we. We only hope that this study of the electronic mirage informs those who might have been susceptible to it. and not only the public, but disinterested astrologers—they do exist—who, as honest albeit naive practitioners, would see in such commercial enterprises the future quick-check of astrology.

Notes

1. This is not the company's true name. But it could have easily chosen *Ordinamus* as its trademark, for the word is an amalgamation of *ORDINAteur* (computer: NT) and *NostradaMUS* (c.f. Chapter 8 above: NT). In any case, this will be its name in this chapter.

2. See my article "L'Astrolgue paré de l'IBM," in *Science et Vie:* 611 (August, 1968), pp. 80–89. I would like to thank the editors of *Science et Vie* for permission to reprint the relevant parts of the study.

3. And we would risk the same misadventure that happened to a young journalist a few years ago. The astrologer presented astonishingly truthful portraits of some celebrities—whose birthdates he had stored in his archives!

4. *De la psychanalyse a l'astrologie,* Editions du Seuil. Moreover, the astrologer willingly lent his assistance to an experiment organized by the monthly magazine *Lectures pour tous* (July, 1963). In this experiment, the first test submitted to the wisdom of the astrologer was the analysis of the horoscope of Bill Rapin, a famous criminal who died on the scaffold.

5. We would have liked to use some of the older, legendary French criminals, but unfortunately, Ordinamus is only programmed for birthdates after 1890.

6. The interpretation of the Ascendant does not appear in Ordinamus, for example. However, the astrologer himself has written: "The Ascendant sign has as much—if not more—influence than the Sun sign." (*Aries,* p. iv, Le Seuil). This is certainly a problem and in part justifies the misgivings expressed above.

7. Let us note the absurdity of automatically predicting a future of ten years for every purchaser of Ordinamus. If a subject was born in 1890, for example, and buys his Ordinamus in 1976, he would be obliged to live at least until 1986, i.e., 96 years!

8. We are respecting the astrologer's style: "Tends to live under the influence of breaks put on his instinct" or "find a guiding light for his mind" are, to say the least, unexpected expressions. It is true that the "creator of modern astrology" is self-taught in psychology. We therefore cannot expect miracles.

9. Daniel Lagache, *La Jalousie amoureuse,* Vol. II, Presses Universitaires de France.

10. Cited by the *Journal de Geneve,* February 10, 1929.

11. Marcel Boll, *L'Occultisme devant la science,* Presses Universitaires de France, 1951.

12. A Parisian tabloid similar to the *National Enquirer.* NT.

13. Book IV, chapter 2.

14. The astrologer's prudence was also evident when we contacted Ordinamus directly to suggest they cooperate in an experiment. We received a categorical refusal.

15. The real name has been modified.

CHAPTER 7
Nostradamus yesterday and today

Opinion polls and the popularity of specialized books show that personal astrology has a serious competitor for the public's attention in what is called mundane astrology. This branch of astrology deals with the destiny of peoples and nations, with the possibility for peace and war in the future, whether near or distant. The practitioner uses planetary cycles to accomplish these predictions, especially those of the distant planets, whose slowness is supposed to give more weight to their influence. Horoscopes of individuals are replaced by those of nations (the United States was born on July 4, 1776) or of important treaties (the armistice was signed on May 8, 1945). "Transits" of "heavy" (equals slow) planets bring about events for these hypothetical people as they do for physical people.

What is the origin of mundane astrology? It, too, is very ancient. A large part of Ptolemy's *Tetrabiblios* was devoted to a list of terrestrial lands and their planetary governors. But of all the astrologers who predicted the future of the world, the most famous lived in the sixteenth century: Michel de Nostre-Dame, known as Nostradamus. There is a Nostradamus mystery: for more than four centuries, his success has never been disproven. It is a psychological mystery that resides not only in public credulity, but in the personality of Nostradamus himself. This intellectual connivance between the prophet and his audience can still be seen today. Only the names of the seers have changed. Mundane astrology is an important chapter in the astrological novel, and it certainly cannot be silently skipped over.

Nostradamus

The prophet was born in Saint-Rémy-en-Crau in the South of France on December 14, 1503, "around the noon hour." He died in Salon-de-Provence on July 2, 1566. Born into a family of Jewish doctors that had lived in the South for several generations, Nostradamus studied medicine in Montpelier. Afterwards, he practiced medicine while traveling throughout France. He struggled with success against the plague in many places, including Narbonne, Toulouse, and Bordeaux. Soon after, he published a work entitled *Singuliéres recettes pour la santé du corps humain,* and then a book for women, *Traité des fardements.* It included descriptions of "love stones" to attract a lover and "leech cups" to keep them; it also included recipes for young lettuce, jam, and candied ginger, "which are marvellous for frigid women and lazy men."

Nostradamus then moved to Salon-de-Provence, not far from Aix. Although modestly at first, it was in this city that he began to prophesy. His initial successes prompted the astrologer to take the big step. In 1555, he published the first edition of *Propheties de Maîstre Michel de Nostre Dame.* It had enormous success. He soon published an enlarged second edition, dedicated to King Henry II. He then had a stroke of luck: Henry's death "on the field of battle in single combat," as was apparently predicted in one of Nostradamus's quatrains, put the entire court of France at his feet, and in particular, Catherine de Medici, the king's superstitious widow. He was invited to Paris, where he was given the title of doctor-astrologer to the court. During the reign of Charles IX, the king went so far as to pay homage to the prophet in his home of Salon.

Respected by kings during his lifetime, his reputation only increased after his death. Thanks to their mysterious obscurity, thanks to a kind of gibberish that was a mixture of many different languages, his prophecies permitted as many interpretations as one could wish. This is why, four hundred years later, they are still a pythoness of the modern world. At the beginning of each new year, they are interrogated throughout the world. There are hundreds of commentators who, year in and year out, tirelessly discover something to explain even the most insignificant contemporary events in the master's jargon.

In order to understand the skill with which Nostradamus constructed his reputation as a seer, here is a story that is still told about him in Salon:

> Pierrette Baloin, a pretty girl of sixteen years, lived next door to the great man. One evening, while leaving her home on her way to a tryst with a young man, she passed Nostradamus, who was meditating, eyes closed, on his sill.
>
> "Good eventide, Sire Nostradamus," said the young girl fearfully.
>
> "Good eventide, little maiden," he answered, without opening his eyes.
>
> An hour later, upon her return from her amorous encounter—which had been particularly animated that evening—she again passed the prophet. Once again she greeted him:
>
> "Good night, Sire Nostradamus."
>
> "Good night, *little woman*," answered he, still without opening his eyes.
>
> Fortunately, it was too dark for her blushing to be seen.[1]

A gifted astrologer

The centuries contain the essential of Nostradamus's prophetic work. They are ten in number and grouped into quatrains. The preface, dedicated by the prophet to his son César, is a masterpiece of diplomacy and craftiness. Nostradamus immediately informs us that the revelations to follow are what "the Divine Spirit has made known to me, through the revolutions of the stars," and have been made thanks to "continual nightly watches." Nostradamus thus recognizes that he is an astrologer, something that is often denied today by those who seek to make him into a visionary. Edgar Leoni, the author of the most notable analysis of Nostradamus's work yet published, points out that there are more than fifty quatrains in which the prediction contains the notation of precise planetary positions.[2] For example:

> The year that Saturn will be conjoined in Aquarius
> With the Sun, the very powerful King
> Will be received and anointed at Reims and Aix,
> After conquests he will murder the innocent.
>
> (IV, 86)

But Nostradamus the astrologer was well aware of the dangers of the Holy Inquisition, in whose opinion those who interrogated the planets were "in commerce with the Devil." He emphasizes in the Preface that "all is regulated and governed by the incalculable power of God, inspiring us not through drunken fury, nor by frantic movement, but through the influences of the stars." In emphasizing this passage, Serge Hutin writes: "The scenes and episodes suddenly foreseen by the magus while under the influence of a supernatural inspiration are always rigorously inserted into astrological cycles."

A psychological analysis of the quatrains that follow the Preface is instructive. One discovers the key to Nostradamus's fascination, like that of his modest successors in later times. Sometimes consciously and often unconsciously, the specialists in world astrology pull the same strings as he. We would say that they use the same archetypes with a more "scientific" language. Let us examine them.

The Cassandra complex: It takes its name from the Trojan woman who unceasingly predicted the most dreadful catastrophes for her fellow countrymen. For Nostradamus, the prediction of the worst catastrophes always leaves a choice. For example:

> Cries, weeping, tears will come with knives,
> Seeming to flee, they will deliver a final attack,
> Parks around to set up high platforms,
> The living pushed back and murdered instantly.

(X, 82)

It is certainly true that the future often holds "cries, weeping, and tears."

Extreme vagueness is the second of Nostradamus's peculiarities. One example among many is:

> In the realm the great one of the great realm reigning,
> Through force of arms the great gates of brass
> He will cause to open, the King and Duke join,
> Fort[3] demolished, ship to the bottom, day serene.

(X, 80)

What is this "realm the great one of the great realm reigning"? Is it Charlemagne, Louis XIV, or Napoleon? As in a rummage sale, you can find here what you are willing to put in. Here is another prediction that makes demands on the reader's powers of discernment:

The end of wolf, lion, ox, and ass,
Timid deer they will be with mastiffs:
No longer will the sweet manna fall upon them,
More vigilance and watch for the mastiffs.

(X, 99)

Could it not even be an anticipation of La Fontaine's fables?
The False Precision is the third aspect of Nostradamian art:

Jupiter and Saturn in the head of Aries,
Eternal God, what changes!
Then for a long age his wicked time returns,
Gaul and Italy, what disturbance.

(I, 51)

Jupiter conjunction Saturn in the Ram (Aries) is a precise astrological configuration, and one that is not often seen. But is it remarkable to associate it with the fact that this conjunction will later
bring about many "changes" and "disturbances" in France (Gaul)
and Italy?

Magic keys: they are constantly used by the master of Salon. An
example is the magic number 7, used throughout the text (seven
days, seven months, seven centuries, seven beasts, seven heads, and
so forth). There is also the evil attached to the passage from one
millenium to the next, something well known since the year 1000.
This is the pretext for one of Nostradamus's rare *dated* predictions
(July, 1999):

The year 1999, seventh month,
From the sky will come a great King of Terror.

(X, 72)

The great terror of the year 1000 that was supposed to mark the
end of the world is found again in the mind of the magus, thinking
ahead to the year 2000.

The successes of Nostradamus

In spite of everything, according to certain specialists, the predictions of our author are so remarkable that one would need an un-
commonly large dose of bad faith to deny their probing validity. Let
us open this golden book of quatrains with its magical marvels, for

they constitute the secular framework of the Nostradamian tradition.

The death of Henry II

The young lion will overcome the old one
On the field of battle in single combat:
He will put out his eyes in a cage of gold:
Two fleets one, then to die a cruel death.   (I, 35)

It is known that during Nostradamus's lifetime, his contemporaries saw in these lines the death of King Henry II, on July 10, 1559. For the defenders of the *Prophéties,* there is no doubt about the prediction: "The fatal event is described here with hallucinating precision: the tournament where Henry II and Montgomery met; the martial game that soon ended in horror (the long lance that penetrated the eyehole of the *golden helmet* worn by the sovereign); the unfortunate Henry II, eyes punctured, suffering horribly for two whole days."[4] The nuanced and documented opinion of Edgar Leoni is the opposite of this enthusiastic interpretation: "The standard interpretation has Montgomery as the young lion and Henry II as the old lion, because both used lions as their emblems. But Buget (1863) points out that Henry II (age forty) was probably only six years older than his adversary (whose exact age is uncertain), that neither one actually used a lion as an emblem, and that the helmet of the king was neither gold nor gilded. . . ." In fact, concludes Leoni, "poetic license would make only lines 1 and 2 substantially acceptable. Line 3 is more dubious. The wound not only did not put out the royal eye, but hardly touched the eye itself. A splinter lodged above his right eye and broke the veins of the pia mater. Line 4 is a complete failure. There was only one wound (unless an abscess be counted) and not two. One might further ad that with *classe* meaning 'fleet' everywhere else in its many occurrences in the *Centuries,* it is rather suspicious to use a Greek derivation here. The most important of all reasons for rejecting this interpretation is that Nostradamus had big things in store for Henry II as the new Charlemagne."[5]

The birth of Napoleon

This prediction is supposedly found in I, 60:

An emperor will be born near Italy
One who will cost his Empire a high price:

They will say that from the sort of people who surround him
He is to be found less prince than butcher.

In fact, "it can be applied equally well to a Holy Roman Emperor (which Nostradamus probably meant), such as Ferdinand II (1619–37), who was born at Graz, about ninety miles from Italy, and surrounded himself with a people like Wallenstein in the Thirty Years War, which certainly cost the Empire dearly." In our opinion, the prediction can also be applied to Hitler, born in Austria near Italy, and who was certainly "less prince than butcher."

The Spanish Civil War

The sixteenth quatrain of *Century IX* struck those who saw the fascist ideology faced with the "great gulf" (of communism):

Out of Castelfranco will come the assembly,
The ambassadors not agreeable will cause a schism:
Those of Riviera will be in the squabble,
And they will refuse entry to the great gulf.

The triumph of General Franco (Castel Franco) with the aid of "those of Riviera"—that is, the partisans of Primo de Rivera—seems to be written in black and white. They are careful to write *castel Franco* and not *Castelfranco*. For there are several cities named Castelfranco and one named Riviera *in Italy,* and not in Spain. The only reasonable question is to wonder which one Nostradamus had in mind: near Modena there is a Castelfranco less than a hundred miles from Riviera. Some see General Franco in *Castelfranco,* as others have seen Hitler in the word *Hister* (frequent in Nostradamus's work). But *Hister* means Danube.

The escape of Louis XVI

Let us read the twentieth quatrain of *Century IX.*

By night will come through the forest of "Reines,"
Two couples roundabout route Queen the white stone,
The monk king gray in Varennes:
Elected Capet causes tempest, fire, blood, slice.

The king's attempted escape and the family's fate are supposedly inscribed in these four lines. The fourth line is quite striking, the final world *slice* recalling the guillotine if one accepts the *cap* as an aberration for Capet.[6] But outside of this, there is little that recalls the pitiful adventure of the king. Everything rests on the name of Varennes: "The name of the small city clearly figures in the quatrain, and it is truly impossible to invoke simple chance: let us repeat that from the historical point of view, nothing important ever happened in this locale, except for the arrest of the fleeing king," writes Hutin.[7] But for his part, Leoni states that there are thirty-six towns named Varennes in France, and one would have to be certain if the gentleman from Salon had Varennes-en-Argonne in mind. We could ask if there is a "Reines" forest on the road from Paris to Varennes. There is not. It does however, pass through the Argonne forest. Perhaps some scholar can find a derivation of Argonne from some word meaning "queen" (Reine) in some language. It would be an interesting proof in Nostradamus's favor.

Nostradamus and the Nazis

Jean de Kerdéland writes: "The book of Prophecies is an inexhaustible magic hat from which modern prestidigitators can pull innumerable rabbits."[8] There are also those who discover in the *Centuries* many contemporary events. General DeGaulle has been seen in it several times. His admirers find him in expressions like: "the valiant personage" (II:14) and "the great legislator" (5, 79). His adversaries are more content with recognizing him in the thirty-fifth quatrain of Century VII where a "great fishery" is discussed.

But not all of the commentators of Nostradamus have been harmless "prestidigitators." Several times, the *Centuries* have been used knowingly and cynically by politicians who sought to turn public opinion in their favor. In 1649, Cardinal Mazarin's enemies had published a counterfeit copy of the *Centuries* that contained apocryphal quatrains directed against the cardinal. But the most tragic avatar to befall the texts of the old master of Salon was their encounter with the Nazis. Goebbels, the propaganda minister of the Third Reich, wrote one day in his diary: "Astrologers in the United States are predicting a premature end for the Führer. We are quite familiar with this type of propaganda, since we have often used it ourselves. As soon as possible, we will once again exploit the possibilities it offers. I count on this having significant results, particularly in the United States and England. . . . We will therefore enlist the services of specialists in prediction of all kinds. Once again, Nostradamus will have to submit to being quoted."[9] Unfortunately for him, Krafft, one of the most famous astrologers of his day, became one of these diligent "specialists."

Karl Ernst Krafft

Who was this Krafft, sometimes called "Hitler's astrologer"? A careful study by Ellic Howe, recently published in England, separates the truth and the legend that surrounds the life and death of this famous astrologer (*Urania's Children,* Kimbler, 1967).

Krafft was born in Basel, Switzerland, on May 10, 1900, into a sturdy, middle-class family. From 1919 to 1923 he studied at the University of Basel, and then at the University of Geneva. It was at this time that he had the idea of statistically proving the validity of astrology. "The tragedy," writes Howe, "was that Dr. Liebmann Hirsch, a professor of statistics at the University of Geneva, thought that Krafft had succeeded in establishing the statistical proof of the existence of astral influences on man." It has now been demonstrated that Krafft was mistaken (c.f. above, Chapter 5), but it is certain that this no doubt lightly given approval pursued Krafft all his life. For from that day forward, so convinced was he of having made a fundamental discovery that he lost all sense of proportion.[10] A dynamic, ambitious man, sure of himself almost to the level of paranoia, Krafft became known to the public, and even created a school of so-called *Typocosmy,* a blend of astrology, philosophy, and psychology. He soon came to scorn Switzerland, his birthland, for he was not received as he thought he should be, and he became fascinated by Hitler (and Nazism) with whom he seems to have shared certain theories on race. He believed that only an authoritarian government like that of the Third Reich could appreciate his true value. When war broke out in 1939, he took up residence in the Black Forest. There he wrote his surprising *Traité d'astrobiologie,* which we discussed above (in Chapter 5). Most of all however, he began to devote himself to deciphering the prophecies of Nostradamus. The choice of Germany as the refuge of his ambition sealed his fate. Destiny came to him in the form of a successful prediction.

Krafft had written confidentially to a certain Dr. Fiesel that in his opinion, Hitler was threatened by an assassination attempt in the first ten days of November, 1939. Then on November 9, 1939, a bomb exploded in the Burgerbräu beerhall in Munich a few minutes after the Führer, anxious to return to Berlin, had left the building. Krafft could not resist the temptation to extol his own powers and could find no better way to do so than to send a telegram to the Reichschancellerie in Berlin to inform them of his success. In Berlin, his telegram "exploded like a second bomb." The embarrassed Dr. Fiesel was summoned first, and had to admit that he had indeed received a letter from Krafft before the blast. Then Krafft himself was summoned. The Gestapo wanted to know if he was really a "seer," or if he was involved in the plot. If he had not already a certain amount of influence, Krafft would certainly have been arrested. But he came to the attention of the Gestapo and became a candidate for certain of Goebbels's projects. At the end of December, 1939, Krafft was summoned to Berlin for the principal purpose of commenting on the prophecies of Nostradamus. He thus came into contact with Dr. Frank, the gauleiter of Poland who would be hung at Nuremburg, and Dr. Ley, who would commit suicide before the verdict. Krafft eagerly undertook the task assigned to him, seeking to read in the *Centuries* the victory of the "new order." He had been told to proceed with the greatest discretion. But Krafft was too proud and too imprudent to be silent about what he believed he was illuminating in the *Centuries*. The Gestapo feared that he might be playing both sides against the middle and that he might be using Nostradamus for the benefit of England as well as Germany. A letter from Krafft to Mr. Tilea, a Rumanian diplomat exiled in London, was intercepted; it explained his work on the Prophecies. The Gestapo demanded that this letter be rewritten in a way that would be completely favorable to German propaganda. But the story of Krafft's letter to Tilea did not stop there. It is said that when the Rumanian received the letter dictated by the Gestapo, he was convinced that Krafft had become a Nazi agent, and told this to an English journalist-astrologer, Capt. Louis de Wohl. After the war, the latter claimed to have caught Krafft and the Nazis composing a counter-interpretation of the Prophecies. But this is probably not true, according to Howe. On the contrary, what is difficult to imagine today, is that there was an effervescence that reigned in the office of psychological warfare once the name of Nostradamus was mentioned. "In his *Memoires*, Walter Schellenberg (the chief of Nazi counter-espionage) relates that in mid-May, 1940, when the German armies were crossing the border at Sedan, he had received an order to cooperate with the Ministry of Propaganda in the preparation and distribution in France by radio and leaflets much "black" material. His office had prepared texts containing frightening quatrains, adapted to the circumstances and taken from the Prophecies. They were dropped from airplanes."[11] Other tracts distributed in

France and Belgium predicted the imminent fall of England in dog-
gerel verse attributed to Nostradamus. Furthermore, it was in 1940
that Krafft's book on the prophecies of Nostradamus was published
in several countries, notably in Portugal and South America. In his
book, Howe reproduces a facsimile of the German edition that was
published in Frankfurt-am-Main in 1940. It was published with the
financial assistance of Himmler's office. Although it has not been
formally established, Krafft's participation in these enterprises is
probable. Let us note in passing that although he was greatly ex-
ploited by the propagandists of some countries, Nostradumus was
taboo in others. In France, the Vichy government prohibited the
sale of the Prophecies of Maistre Michel Nostradamus, edited by a
certain Dr. Fontbrune, for fear that the commentaries would shock
the occupying armies. As for the prudent Switzerland, in 1940, it
only permitted a republication of the 1649 edition of the Prophecies
that did not even contain a translation of the text in modern French!

During this time, Krafft was in Berlin, continuing to interpret
the magus of Salon and giving consultations and lectures. He even
published a small, confidential journal entitled *Nostra Damur.*

It was at this time—May 10, 1941—that Hitler's Crown Prince,
Rudolph Hess, decided to flee to England. One of the leading figures
in Germany, Hess was also the great protector of the astrologers.
Hitler's rage turned against them, and they were pursued and arrested. Krafft did not escape the Führer's vengeance, and was imprisoned on a charge of espionage on June 12, 1941. At the beginning, his status was still that of a forced laborer. But little by little,
the situation deteriorated. Becoming more and more eccentric,
Krafft could do nothing to arrange things. He was absolutely unaware of the fate that awaited him. In spite of the efforts of his wife,
he was sent to Oranienburg in December 1944, and then to Buchen-
wald. But he never reached the infamous concentration camp, dying
en route on January 8, 1945. And so he died, a victim of his too-
exclusive love for Nostradamus, of his admiration of the New Order,
of his pride, and of his boastfulness, he who was called "Hitler's
astrologer" and who died under the boot of the Gestapo.

Once an obstacle tripped an astrologer
Who fell into a well. The neighbors said,
"Poor fool! You can't see what's underfoot and you a seer.
How do you read the stars above your head?"[12]

This prophetic quatrain comes not from Nostradamus, but from
La Fontaine.

Nostradamus today

Let us leave behind the master of Salon and his legend. Let us discuss the astrologers who have followed the same path. There are still several Nostradamuses in the twentieth century. At year's end, the media seeks out their predictions on what the heavenly bodies portend for the new year. Books that give even more precise revelations are regularly published. The sixteenth-century spirit is in perfect health today. The psychology of the practitioner has not changed. It is worth the trouble to give a few examples of predictions by modern magi, predictions that are enigmatic and serious, falsely precise or sensible. At the same time, we shall question the validity of contemporary mundane astrology.

The Cassandras

There is an overabundance of catastrophe prediction among modern astrologers. And the example of Nostradamus is there to encourage them. For the more horrors that are predicted, the more the public's imagination is struck. In his "Predictions for 1962," here is what one of the best-known of this breed stated: "The end of the Fifth Republic in France; the return of Jacques Soustelle[13]; partial mobilization in Holland; proclamation of a republic of Iran; a singular epidemic in the Middle East; the fall of Nassar; serious, very serious (underlined) developments in Israel; several kingdoms will fall; a dreadful famine in China," and so on.

Here is another example taken as well from an astrologer of great renown. At the end of 1963, he published a book entitled *La Crise mondiale de 1965*. Did anyone else state that that year was a "new critical stage in the history of the world"? No one. "A Norwegian with a computer and time to waste calculated the number of wars since the beginning of recorded history. He counted 14,531. During a period of 5,560 years, the average was 2.6 wars per year. Since 1945, the planet has been afflicted with more than 40 wars."[14] Since 1945, war has been permanent. But contrary to the pessimistic predictions of the astrologer, 1965 was an "average" year, with one episodic war—between India and Pakistan over Kashmir—and another endemic one—in Vietnam, which had been going on since 1959. Furthermore, as Jacques Garai notes, the war in Vietnam was one of the nongeneralized conflicts that specialists call "medium tension wars."

The persistent

These great tenors of world astrology seem quite imprudent. But they know how short the memory of their public is. Thus they do not hesitate to repeat the same prediction any number of times, convinced that one day it will come true. One of the best examples is that of the end of the war in Algeria. The first astrological prediction dates from January, 1958. The astrologer wrote in a magazine: "Will the war in Algeria be over by All Saints Day in 1958?" But alas, it had not ended by November 1. This did not discourage the practitioner—or rather the charlatan—however; and in the *same magazine* he wrote in October 1959, that "perhaps it would end around December 5, 1959." When the soldiers apparently ignored his call, the astrologer persevered: "Towards an armistice?" he asked in May, 1960, *still in the same magazine.* This time he offered a choice of "new forces towards peace" around February 15, June 20, and July 16, 1960. Three dates were printed in large type, three dates when nothing important happened. Moreover, the insurrection of January 24, 1960, gave new impetus to the Algerian conflict. But the damned war had to end one day, and this time serious rumors of peace were circulating. Thus the astrologer continued his predictions, writing in March, 1961, the triumph of persistence: "The closest peaceful wave can be seen for the beginning of 1962, in January and February." In fact, the cease fire was declared on March 18. The astrologer had had to revise his predictions several times, and only partially succeeded when the end of the war had become inevitable. What does it matter! He waved this "success" like a flag in his later writings, and for his audience, his attitude is certainly justified.[15]

The sages

It seems clever to predict "sensibly" in the direction of the greatest probability. In 1963, an astrologer entitled his article "France: The End of Gaullism?" He was not unaware of the fact that power can be depleted, and that General DeGaulle was aging. "If one limits oneself to the classic rules of traditional astrology," he wrote, "DeGaulle will not die a natural death [This was the period of attempts on the General's life.]. . . . Whether it is because of an illness or an accident—the first being more probably [DeGaulle was advancing in years.], *the departure of the President of France from political life will thus be found during the year 1965.*[16]

In the same exciting book, the astrologer confides to us that "it is very possible that John F. Kennedy will be re-elected to the American presidency in November, 1964." A logical prediction that an ex-Marine caused to fail. Later in the same instructive epistle we read: "In 1965, Khrushchev ... will have some very strong trump cards, and will obtain a sure result." Alas, before the time fixed by the astrologer for him to "rise to the pinnacle of prestige and popularity, Khrushchev was overthrown (in October, 1964). The hazards of history deceived the astrologer's sensible predictions.

The imprecise

Here is a banal case taken from a popular astrological magazine. It deals with predictions for France for the month of February, 1968: "Diplomatic circles and relationships with bordering countries will probably be affected by the Saturn quincunx Neptune. It is not impossible that a friendly nation will lodge a protest against our country in a high assembly. . . . Accidents or spectacular deaths will occur in artistic circles," and so on. Since each month has its cortege of diplomatic incidents and accidents, only exact dates and names would have a probing force. But no, like his illustrious ancestor, the magus prefers to remain vague. Speaking of Vietnam, he tells us that "the intensification of the war will continue inexorably. The adversaries will trade attacks and pitiless reprisals." Although he did not greatly exert his imagination, the astrologer numbered this prediction among his great successes some months later.

The halo effect

What is the effect of these predictions on their audience? From the astrologer's point of view it is the best. Catastrophes and little news items feed the imagination of the crowds and the portfolio of the practitioners. Mundane astrology is a solid bread-winner that has no bad years. It uses everything that happens in the world. The death of John F. Kennedy, for example, proved to be a profitable windfall. Several astrologers have built a part of their fortunes on President Kennedy's tragic demise. It is almost surprising that one of them did not print on his business cards, "X. Predicted the death of Kennedy." He did not do this, although he must have thought about it, for he regularly states it in advertisements.

A well-known psychological phenomenon called the halo effect is often used by astrologers to their advantage. Part of a prediction possesses a particularly striking affective resonance. These words then project their halo over the whole prediction in the reader's mind. One can see how Nostradamus's commentators have been the victims of a halo effect in Century IX, 20. Clouding critical sense, the word *Varennes* played this key role. There are numerous modern examples where the version of a prediction is progressively simplified in the astrologer's favor when it circulates among followers of astrology. This is another aspect of astrological testimony that our study tried to uncover in the case of individual astrology.

Taking over for science

But why should the astrologer be the one to monopolize the future of the planet? In fact, science knows more about our future today than the wildest dreams of any astrologer. Psychology, sociology, genetics and statistics direct and clarify chance. In December,1965, eight days before the presidential election in France the French Public Opinion Institute predicted the exact percentage of votes that DeGaulle was to receive. No fortune-teller managed to do so. The achievement is not by fortune-tellers then, but by the technology of public opinion surveys. Is there not something miraculous in the prediction of the behavior of twenty million voters by interrogating only a few thousand? It is the triumph of the laws of chance over the anti-chance of the astrologers. Even the future of the world can be scientifically predicted, thanks to the use of computers. There is no need for Nostradamus here. Using technology to foresee the future has become an important part of the work of many avant-garde scientific laboratories. In the United States, these ideas are already being applied. The Rand Corporation has recently published a wide panorama of the principal discoveries of mankind in the future. Even an approximate date has been given. Robert W. Prehoda, a researcher in Los Angeles, is considered to be one of the pioneers of this methodology of the future. Nostradamus would not disclaim the title of Prehoda's book, published in 1967, *Designing the Future*[17]; but the sub-title—*The Role of Technicological Forecasting*—would astonish the old master. In France, a plan has been created to forecast the economic and social expansion of our country in the years to come.

But . . . proud science, the tamer of chance, will sometimes be opposed by anti-chance. The historical texture of peoples and the careers of great men are sometimes shaken by dramas that no science in today's world is capable of predicting. What computer could have told John F. Kennedy not to take the plane to Dallas in 1963, or his brother Robert not to go to Los Angeles in 1968? What computer could have diagnosed the extraordinary social agitation that shook France in May, 1968? History's great indicators still withhold their mysteries, and philosophers try to penetrate them. But in vain. In their own way, the Nostradamuses of yesterday and today fill the gaps in our knowledge. They exert a social function that, for as much as it appears to us as indigenous to twentieth century man, does not tranquilize the public any less. Two wars per year: this reminds us, it is true, that above our heads there is a sword of Damocles.

Notes

1. Jean de Kerdéland, *De Nostradamus à Cagliostro,* Self, 1945.

2. Edgar Leoni, *Nostradamus: Life and Literature,* Nosbooks, 1961.

3. Var. port.

4. Hutin, *op cit.*

5. *Classe*—"fleet" in the last line is often translated as "wound," from the Greek *klasis.* NT).

6. In French, the last line begins "Elu cap, cause tempête . . . . " (NT).

7. *Op cit.,* p. 56.

8. *Op cit.*

9. Lochner, *The Goebbels Diaries,* London, 1948, pp. 142, 145.

10. Cf.also Howe, *Astrology: a recent history including the untold story of its role in W.W.II,* New York, Walker, 1968 (NT).

11. Howe, *op cit.*

12. Eng. Trans. M. Moore.

13. A French politician who did not return before 1972 (NT).

14. Jacques Garai, *Candide,* December, 1965.

15. The predictions are found in *Cahiers Astrologiques* in January, 1958, November, 1959, May, 1960, and March, 1961.

16. The italics are the astrologer's. And we might remember DeGaulle did not leave office until 1969 and died in November, 1970.

13. Chilton Book Company, New York.

CHAPTER 8
Cosmic influence

However it is judged, astrology loses in serious confrontations. Even if they are cast by renowned practitioners, the individual horoscope and the world prediction appear scientifically as nonsense. Thus there would be nothing more to say, astrology would be only deceit and deception, and the heavenly bodies would have no influence on man.

Nevertheless it is certainly the sun that warms and gives life to the earth, and the moon and sun controls tides. Certain heavenly bodies have a discernible influence. The demonstration of the illusions of traditional horoscope does not prohibit the study of this influence or of cosmic effects as yet unknown to science, but whose reality will perhaps be verified one day. The time has come in the present work to undertake a constructive task, one far from all sectarianism and all superstition.

Houses twelve and nine

Our verifications of what astrologers call houses has been kept for the end. The problem is a difficult one. It demands a complex methodology and the hour of birth must be known. If valid statistics for houses are to be established, one is obliged to maintain a long and difficult correspondence with civil registries in thousands of towns and cities. Most authors have backed away from such a task. This is why few, very few studies that seek to examine the reality of houses have been published.

It will be remembered that the twelve houses are supposed to arbitrarily represent the factors of daily life. The second house, for example, informs us about money, the fifth house about pleasures and spectacles, the tenth house about professional success, and so on.[1] One of these factors can be chosen and examined with the help of statistics. Let us take the example of professional success: it is a relatively simple matter to gather a set of individuals that are representative of the major occupations and to observe the frequency of one planet in the tenth house. This is what we have done. The French astrologer Choisnard stated that the presence of the benefic Jupiter in the tenth house was frequent for those who succeeded in life and were covered with honors. The observation of such a result would have confirmed one of traditional astrology's allegations.

We assembled a considerable number—more than 16 thousand in all—of birth dates of famous people. But there was no marked accumulation of those who were born with Jupiter in the tenth house. It is the same for the other planets. Nothing in the traditional horoscope permits the prediction of professional success in its whole.

All the same, there was a surprise for us when we examined the great wheel of fortune of the twelve astrological houses: there were significant numbers in two of them, the ninth and twelfth houses. Astrological tradition calls these regions "cadent houses" and states that planets in these houses can only have a particularly weak and sometimes ill-fated influence. For astronomers, on the other hand, they are regions marked by two crucial points that are carefully calculated in their tables, for they are essential to the observation of the heavenly bodies: the twelfth house follows the *rise* of the planet at the horizon and the ninth house its *culmination,* that is, the highest point in its daily journey. The results we found were too improbable to be explainable by a simple stroke of luck. But they were undeniably opposed to the traditional laws of astrology. The precise meaning given by astrologers was of no help; in fact:

Ninth house: long journeys, religion, philosophy, large animals;

Twelfth house: "the Hell of the zodiac," hidden enemies, prisons, difficulties, diverse illnesses and misfortunes.

Finding significant numbers for planets in these regions of the sky at the birth of well-known people surprises the traditional astrologer as much as the rational scientist. In fact, the contradiction between the pessimistic interpretation of the twelfth house and the striking professional success of the people we examined is quite apparent. On the other hand, if a group of criminals condemned to death is gathered, although it would be expected, there is no significant result in the twelfth house. As for the influences attributed to the ninth house, they are so disparate that it is hardly astonishing that the facts are contradictory.

We have thus replaced the ancient concept of houses with the modern one of *sectors*. They have the same astronomical definition, but are numbered from one to twelve in the direction of the diurnal movement of the heavenly bodies, not in the opposite direction, as is the curious procedure of astrology. The twelfth house becomes sector one, following the rise of the planet, the eleventh house becomes sector two, the tenth house becomes sector three, the ninth house becomes sector four, following the culmination of the planet, and so on.

Planets and professions

The first group of notables to present abnormal frequencies according to the rise and the culmination of certain planets was 676 medical "academicians." In order to be certain that this unexplainable phenomenon was not due to a simple astronomical effect or to a demographic law, we collected a group of ordinary people from official records who were born during the same years as the great doctors. There were none of the anomalies of the group of academicians. Then a second group of famous doctors who had done important research and had written technical books was assembled. We had to submit to the evidence. The same abnormal figures according to the rise and the culminations occurred.[2] There was an incomprehensible relationship between the fact of pursuing a noteworthy medical career and that of being born after the rise or the culmination of certain heavenly bodies. In order to further examine such surprising results, the statistics were extended to other professional notables, whose names were taken from biographical dictionaries from France and from other countries. We requested birth records from France, Italy, Germany, Belgium, and Holland. When the results were tabulated, they still showed the same amazing observations in the two hours that roughly follow the rise and the culmination of certain heavenly bodies.[3] There were extremely marked differences between actual and expected frequencies—among 3,647 scientists and doctors, 724 instead of the 626 (the calculated theoretical number) were born after the rise or the culmination of Mars.[4] There is but one in 500,000 that such an excess is due to chance. For the same group, 704 instead of 598 were born after the rise or culmination of Saturn. The probability of chance: one in three hundred thousand.

—For 3,438 well-known military men, Jupiter and Mars were found to be very frequent in the zones that follow their rise and culmination, Jupiter 703 instead of 572 and Mars 680 instead of 590. The possibility of this being due to chance is less than one in a million.

—Among 2,088 sports champions, Mars alone dominated, but with a surprising statistical clarity. It was found to be rising or culminating 452 times rather than the expected 358 times, which has a probability of chance of one in five million.

—Among 1,409 famous actors, Jupiter was counted 283 times in these regions of the heavens instead of an expected 234. The probability of chance: one in one thousand.

We also observed improbable accumulations for 1,003 political leaders (Jupiter and the moon), 1,352 writers (the moon), 903 journalists (Jupiter), and 202 business leaders (Mars).

But the variations in frequency do not always appear as *more;* occasionally they appeared as *less.* There were cases in which the planets, rather than demonstrating an abnormally strong tendency to appear after the rise or the culmination, had such a small frequency in these regions that there again, the result could not be explained by chance.

Mars and Saturn were rarely found after the rise and the culmination among 2,339 great painters and musicians. For Mars, there were 323 instead of an expected 402, and for Saturn, 321 instead of 378. The probability of this being due to chance in the two cases is less than one in one thousand. The same phenomenon was observed for 1,352 writers.

In the same way, chance cannot explain the significantly small number of scientists born at the rise or the culmination of Jupiter, the small number of sports champions and military men born with the moon in these regions, and so on.

Finally, the possibility of explanation by chance is further diminished by the fact that the results were constantly repeated from one country to another for similar professional groups. Such surprising results could not be accepted without ample verification.[5] Scientists from a variety of disciplines were consulted: statisticians, astronomers, demographers, gynecologists, and physicists. They suggested diverse counter-experiments that could lead to the discovery of types of errors that were possible: partiality in the choice of births, poor understanding of the astronomical or demographic conditions, incorrect use of statistical formulas, and so on. But none of these counter-experiments could account for the recorded results, which resisted every attack.[6]

The "resistance" of this unexplainable fact was interesting enough to the Belgian Committee for the Scientific Investigation of Alleged Paranormal Phenomena (in abbreviation, PARA committee) that they too examined our experiments. This committee, more than a little skeptical, is composed of several scientists from different disciplines. This committee was founded twenty-five years ago in order to verify and, if possible, to demolish some of the scientific claims like ours.

The committee decided not only to examine our research, but to repeat on new material one of our most significant experiments. They examined a group of sports champions, at whose birth Mars was so abnormally distributed in the heavens. Having assembled a new group of 535 sports champions, both French and Belgian, the members of this committee put their data in a computer that had been programmed with the complex movements of Mars. The statistical analysis of the positions of Mars given by the computer showed a greater frequency than expected of this planet after its rise or its culmination at the birth of these 535 champions. At the birth of ordinary people, the same phenomenon does not appear. The PARA committee noted these facts and considered that they posed a true scientific problem. But there were doubts expressed as to the cause that produced this result.[7]

It is not destiny

How can the positions of the planets lead individuals towards certain professions? It seems quite absurd. The profession of bicycle racer, for example, has existed for less than a century, while the planet that would supposedly lead someone to choose this profession has existed for millions of years. Thus the planet does not act on the profession itself. This can be demonstrated. One can gather a group of people who followed the same career as the personalities studied above, but who did not achieve as much fame. Soldiers who did not surpass the lower ranks, businessmen who took over for their fathers but did nothing substantial themselves, actors who remained in the shadows of other stars, and so on. There is no planetary result that appears at the birth of these people in the same profession, but who only had average "success."[8]

The professional label thus does not explain everything, far from it. An element of notoriety must be added. Why? Must the results then be interpreted in terms of a favorable destiny? This as well is not the correct explanation. An example will show why. Among the famous military men in our groups, there are as many remarkable heroes who were killed while they were young as there are generals who often died at a very advanced age. The young heroes certainly had their hour of glory. They were decorated. But their careers were shattered by death or crippling, and they certainly did not profit from the fugitive and often posthumous honors they received. They did not have the good fortune of their comrades to survive the dangers and to later become powerful and respected leaders. The planetary anomalies are nevertheless the same in the two cases. One can deduce from this that our results most assuredly do not reflect good fortune or misfortune, nor any evolution in human destiny that would be the result of favorable or unfavorable chance.

A temperamental tendency

To what do the professional groups that we have examined correspond? To the great categories of human activity: science, art, literature, politics, war, sport, etc. These professions are something completely different from the monotonous exercise of a lucrative activity. Rather they represent characteristic behavior: creating a work of art, making a discovery, playing a role in the theater, or performing some exploit. There are no doubt different ways of pursuing research or winning in a sporting event. But it can be assumed that on the average, certain qualities are almost always indispensable. Since we collected the individuals in our groups from biographical dictionaries, we had the idea of reexamining these same works and consulting the biographies in detail, in order to familiarize ourselves with the usual behavior and character traits of these individuals, according to the testimony of people who knew and studied them. Thus the thousands of people in our groups were examined again, this time from the angle of their personality, and not from that of their profession. A file has been established for each individual, where we noted the judgments published by the historians or the biographers. We then compared them to each individual planetary result.

Let us give an example: Raymond Kopa, one of the greatest French soccer players, was born when Mars had just risen. Now, we read in his biography: "To his exceptional technical abilities, he adds uncommon vivacity, will, and stubbornness." But a single case certainly does not permit a conclusion. Will similar character traits be found in the majority of other people born at the rise or the culmination of the planet Mars? Let us take the biographical work that gave us the birth dates of 570 champions of French sport.[9] Let us examine the judgments of character attributed to 136 of them born after the rising or culmination of Mars. As an example, here are the expressions that occur most often in the description of the character of these 136 champions: "energetic, brave, willful, hard-working, tireless, aggressive, exceptional temperament, quick to make a decision, resolute, great fighter, dynamic, does not mince his words," and so on.

For the sportsmen born at hours when Mars was neither rising nor culminating however, the above qualities rarely appear and in fact, one often finds: "Lack of vigor, a dilletante, inconsistency," etc. Certainly, there are exceptions to this. But analyzed with the calculation of probabilities, the temperamental differences between the Mars group and the non-Mars group are absolutely decisive.

The collection of thousands of biographies in order to extract judgments of character is a long and arduous task. For this reason, it has not been completed for all the professional groups. But the work is in a good state of achieved progress and there are few remaining doubts. The planetary positions observed are linked neither to the profession nor to chance, but to certain personality traits and temperamental dispositions that are quite marked in the notable individuals we have studied.[10]

Genetic sensitivity

Does this mean that a child's temperament is determined by a few astral rays that mark him with an indelible seal? When he enters the world, the child is completely formed by the potential inherited from his parents. It cannot be asserted that the planet acts on the chromosomic structure of the child's cells, that it disrupts and redistributes them to the point of changing his mentality. In reality, the same individual born three weeks earlier would still later become a doctor, a sportsman, or a painter, according to his temperament. This is why we believe that the planet adds nothing to the child that is born, but at the most, is an "indicator" of a temperamental tendency that will later lead him to adopt a career that fits this temperament.

Let us consider once again the example of Raymond Kopa. When he was born in Noeux-les-Mines (France) on December 11, 1931, at 9:00 A.M., Mars had just appeared on the horizon. With what is known today about the genetic transmission of paternal and maternal characteristics, could one imagine even for a moment that if Mars had been in another sector of the sky, Kopa would not have become Kopa? Hereditary disposition linked with a series of favorable environmental circumstances made him into the great champion that he became. If the planet is to be integrated into this circuit, account must be taken of heredity.

Psychology teaches us—and especially the work of Kretchmer, Sheldon, and Eysenck—that there is a hereditary basis to temperamental predisposition. Since the position of the planet indicates a factor of personality, there can be only one explanation: the factor has to be linked to heredity. Thus the position of the planet must also be linked to heredity. If Kopa received an exceptionally combative temperament from nature, one of his parents must probably have exhibited this temperament before him. It can be supposed that this parent was probably born when Mars was rising or culminating.

Planetary heredity

This hypothesis has been confirmed under the name of the "planetary effect in heredity," thanks to a study of more than 30 thousand hours of birth collected from official birth records in Paris and several places in the Parisian area. We noted a tendency for children to come into the world in the same cosmic conditions that prevailed at the births of their parents. More precisely, children have a tendency to be born when a planet rises or culminates, if that same planet was found in the same regions of the heavens at their parents' birth. Certainly, the tendency is not of great amplitude. Taking the large number of births examined into account however, the probability that chance alone produced such similarities from one generation to another is about one in 500 thousand. Nevertheless, the effect appears only with the planets that are closest to the earth or are the most massive: the moon, Venus, Mars, Jupiter, and Saturn, those that can be seen with the naked eye. No hereditary similarity has been observed for the more distant planets—Uranus, Neptune, and Pluto—nor for Mercury, the smallest planet in the solar system.

Other interesting observations have been noted about the planetary effect in heredity. First of all, it is not linked to sex. Hereditary similarities are as frequent between father and children as between mother and children. In the same way, the statistical tendency remains constant for boys and girls. But an important observation must be added: if both parents are born at the rise or the culmination of the *same* planet, the tendency is doubled for the child. There is another result: planetary heredity is diluted through successive generations. Thus everything combines to suggest that the planetary effect in heredity does not contradict the classic laws of modern genetics.[11]

Planetary heredity definitively eliminates the idea of predestination attached to the planets. As Giorgio Piccardi, the director of the Physical Chemistry Institute of the University of Florence, wrote in the Preface to one of our books, "It must not be thought that the action of the heavenly body is fixed forever in the organism of the child who is born. It is a passing thing and only acts during the childbirth itself."[12] The child seems to be endowed with a "planetary sensitivity" that provokes its coming into the world at a preferential moment of the diurnal path of this or that planet. How can this result be explained? It is known that once the moment of birth has come, anything at all can cause labor pains to begin. This "anything" might be partially linked to cosmic factors, the child reacting to a cosmic "instruction" to which his hereditary type might make him more susceptible than to others. Playing the role of catalyst or screen (we do not know at the present time), the planet might thus determine in part the hour of birth triggering the labor. Here is a possible mechanism that seems reasonable to gynecologists at the present time: with birth imminent, the mother's uterine contractions are begun and guided by hormonal secretions that come from the fetal elements. These secretions might themselves be partially stimulated by the diurnal passage of the cosmic "triggering."[13] But what happens when the doctor modifies the normal progression of childbirth, either by surgical intervention or by the introduction of labor-regulating chemicals into the mother's system? The practice of "induced or stimulated labor" has been considerably developed in the last thirty years. We therefore established formal controls: in these cases, the planetary effect disappears. There are no planetary similarities found between parent and child. Medical intervention annihilates the effect of cosmic "instruction." The position of the planet at the birth of children born after induced or stimulated childbirth does not permit us to learn anything about their temperamental type. This is assuredly a bothersome consequence, but at least it has the advantage of illustrating what we said above. The action of the heavenly body has no occult property that plays a direct role without taking into account the natural susceptibility that the child receives from his parents.

The solar field

Such results might have seemed unlikely only twenty years ago. This is no longer completely true today. It was believed that space was a void. In fact, it is full of matter and energy. Space now has another aspect for the astrophysicist. We know that the nearest planets—Venus, Mars, Jupiter, and Saturn—are not mute bodies of rock. In addition to their visible light, they send us other messages. J. A. Roberts, a radioastronomer, noted in 1963 that the planets—and Jupiter in particular—were the source of powerful radio signals received by astronomers with large radio telescopes. The outbursts provoked by these emissions in recording curves are sometimes nearly the equal of those caused by the sun itself. For his part, the French astronomer Treillis communicated to the French Academy of Science his observations on the role played by planetary "tides" on the sun's activity.[14]

Even more recently, artificial satellites have permitted the discovery that the moon and the planets leave a wake behind them, magnetic tails that could bring about disturbances in the solar field. In 1964, the astrophysicists Dessler and Bowen calculated that the length of the earth's magnetospheric tail was equal to at least twenty times the distance from the earth to the sun. All these trails left in the solar field probably produce complex interactions. We begin to get a glimpse of the disturbing role that they exert on terrestrial magnetism, and maybe, consequently, on us.

If, in spite of everything, the planets do not have a sufficient, direct influence on us, the sun does. When it is covered with sunspots, for example, it disrupts compasses and makes radio communication impossible: the earth's magnetism is measurably disturbed, and it is said that there is a magnetic storm. A hypothesis is possible: planetary effect is not exerted directly on us, but rather it passes through the solar field. If this were the case, the effect would be influenced by the varying activity on the sun, or if you prefer, by the varyingly marked agitation of terrestrial magnetism. This is in fact what we observed in a reexamination of our groups of births. The planetary effect in heredity is statistically twice as strong on the days that the geomagnetism is disturbed as on days when it is quiet.

Here then the influence of the planets is no doubt reduced to more reasonable proportions: they seem to act very little or not at all by themselves but probably only modulate the action of solar flows that reach us. The sun is probably the origin of all the planetary effects observed at birth. The planetary effect doubtlessly still remains very mysterious. But thanks perhaps to our last observations on the geomagnetism it is no longer *too* mysterious in the eyes of some men of science.

Furthermore, many of them think that there is a whole world of cosmic influences that remain to be discovered. At the Second International Symposium on the Relationships between Solar and Terrestrial Phenomena in Physical Chemistry and Life Sciences in which we participated, a hundred scientists from every discipline presented their observations. Electromagnetic phenomena of solar, lunar, or planetary origin would have subtle and unexpected effects on human beings. The studies of G. Piccardi of Florence University and C. Capel-Boute of Brussels University on chemical reactions, those of Frank A. Brown of Northwestern University on animals, as well as many others, justify the following remark made by Professor Piccardi: "It is not necessary for us to project a man into interplanetary space, or even for him to leave his country or his house, in order to subject him to the effects of the cosmos. Man is always in the middle of the universe, for the universe is everywhere."[15] We have described Piccardi's exciting discoveries in other books, and we shall not return to them here, except to point out their scientific kinship with our own research.[16]

The confrontation with astrology

In order to compare them with the traditional doctrine of astrology, it is no doubt interesting to briefly summarize the whole of our results. Verification with statistics demonstrates that the symbolism of the houses is illusory; but there is an unexplainable increase of planetary positions in the ninth and twelfth houses in relation to brilliant professional success. These portions of the heavens are considered by the astrologers to be "cadent"—that is, of a weak or bad influence.

It has been demonstrated that contrary to astrological tradition, this planetary effect has no role in the fortune or misfortune of individuals. On the contrary, it seems to be in relationship with their biological temperament, and it is the latter that permits them to succeed in a professional activity for which they show themselves to be particularly suited. Their profession is but a convenient criterion used to establish extensive statistics, but it is their personality that accounts for the observed planetary effect.

We reject the classical astrological hypothesis of an astral influence that would be added to heredity and hence determine the temperament of the child. Modern science teaches us that this is impossible. The planetary effect seems only to provoke birth at a given moment, as a function of a kind of "planetary sensitivity" that the child inherits from his parents. It is a hypothesis confirmed by the discovery of a planetary effect in heredity between parents and children. Revealed in this way during the crisis of childbirth, cosmic influence seems until now to be limited to this first moment of existence. At most, the planet plays as a "trigger effect" for provoking the birth, and it bears witness to the type of temperament that the child has inherited from his parents.

It is finally realized that the planets probably do not act directly and by themselves, as the astrologers naively imagined. They are probably only responsible for still unknown disturbances that modify the primordial action of the sun. The relationship between planetary effects and geomagnetic disturbances—themselves conditioned by solar activity—gives a rather decisive proof that our system's star might be the most important cause of the observed effects. And we know that the effects of the sun on our globe is a scientific object of study admitted by all researchers.

Thus each time that some progress was made in the under standing of the initial aberrant result encountered during an examination of astrological theses, it put a little more distance between us and the astrologers. When a possible astrological interpretation presents itself, it must give way to a hypothesis that is more in agreement with contemporary science. One day an astrologer put the question frankly: "Gauquelin has achieved undeniable results with indubitably astrological material. It remains to ask if these results have an astrological nature." Men of science were not mistaken. For them it is a question of a new effect of the cosmic ambiance, one that is still very mysterious and difficult to explain, but whose physical reality surely owes nothing to occultism. The organizers of several international scientific colloquia have asked us to present our research.[17] As for the still numerous points of obscurity, we hope that step by step they will be clarified, as a function of the progress in science and the advancing of our research.

This said, we can comfortably recognize that it is an astrological idea to associate the position of the planets and the birth moment. Curiously, this idea is founded in truth. More so: a superficial examination of our results seems to present a sketchy confirmation to the ancient astrological symbolism. The planet Mars, the symbol of the god of war, is dominant among military men; the planet Saturn, traditionally leading to a reflective life, appears for scientists; the moon is frequent among poets. But however intriguing this sketch may be, it cannot be completed. The symbolism of the other planets in the solar system is not demonstrated by statistics. The sun does not appear among the leaders (military, political, etc.); nor Venus for artists (musicians, painters, actors); nor Mercury for writers and businessmen. Jupiter, considered traditionally as a stable, "middle-class" planet, is abnormally strong among the great Nazi dignitaries. And none of the more distant planets—Uranus, Neptune, and Pluto—justifies the symbolism that modern astrologers have lightly attributed to them.

The few "rediscovered" symbols perhaps are the result of a fortuitous coincidence rather than a veritable "intuition" by the ancients. But this "intuition" is not impossible. To explain it, one could envisage a kind of empirical signification acquired during long practice and that would have been drowned under a jumble of imaginary observations. In our opinion, to reserve this possibility is to adopt the most impartial attitude—and therefore the most scientific—towards a strange phenomenon that we are just beginning to understand today. Certain scientists have been "saddened" by the very few points of likeness between our results and astrological tradition; while for their part, the believers in this tradition reproach us for removing the planetary effect in heredity too far from the domain of pure astrology. But is modern chemistry called alchemy or the medicine of century called sorcery? Often this science is born in magic and superstition, although it is neither magic nor superstition. One cannot change the facts so that they can be more easily wedded to a prefabricated mode of thought. We must subject ourselves to the judgment of observation. That a diagnosis of the hereditary temperament of child is possible once one knows the planet that rises or culminates at the hour of birth is an assertion heavy with consequence. It is a fact that deserves to be verified, examined in depth, explained, or contradicted by all those who are not content with comfortable illusions, but who are ready to make a few sacrifices in order to extract one more secret from nature.

Notes

1. See Chapter Three above.

2. M. Gauquelin, *L'Influence des astres, étude critique et expérimentale,* Lab. d'ét. des Relations entre Rythmes Cosmiques et Psychophysiologiques, Paris, 1955.

3. M. Gauquelin, *Les Hommes et les astres,* Denoël, Paris, 1960.

4. More precisely, with the planet situated in sector one or four (the twelfth and ninth houses for the astrologers).

5. In 1970–71, we published all the birth and planetary data of professional groups we gathered in 6 volumes (Series A, Vol. 1–6); another book (Series C, Vol. 1) gives the statistical results (Laboratoire d'étude des Relations entre Rythmes Cosmiques et Psychophysiologiques, 8 rue Amyot 75005 Paris, France).

6. For his part, the French specialist on this question Paul Couderc, astronomer at the Paris Observatory has never indicated any errors in our investigations.

7. The problem is in fact astonishingly complex. In order to predict what probability Mars has of appearing in any given region of the heavens, it is necessary to take into account the declination of the planet on that day, as well as the hourly frequency of the moment of birth, the angle between Mars and the sun, and so on. See our book *"Methodes pour etudier les astres dans le mouvement diurne"(1957),* and the debate published in several issues of *The Humanist* since 1975.

8. See *"Les Hommes et les Astres"* 1960, pp. 162–63.

9. *L'Athlège,* Kleber Editions (1949 and 1950).

10. Four volumes have been published in our "Psychological Monographs Series" (Series C, Volumes 2–5); The Mars Temperament and Sports Champions, The Saturn Temperament and Men of Science, The Jupiter Temperament and Actors, The Moon Temperament and Writers (Lab. d'ét. des Relations entre Rythmes Cosmiques et Psycholphysiologiques, Paris 1973–74).

11. M. Gauquelin, *L'Hérédité planetaire,* Denoł, Paris, 1966. Our laboratory published in six volumes all the birth and planetary data gathered for this hereditary experiment (Series B, Vol. 1–6, 1970–71). We recently presented the result of a new experiment in heredity on 35 thousand new cases of parents and children. The same planetary effect has been observed as for our first inquiry (7th International Interdisciplinary Cycle Research Symposium, Bad Homburg, Germany, 1976).

12. *Ibid.,* p. 17.

13. Medical science today thinks that it is the fetus itself that cues in the moment of birth through a hormonal mechanism. A symposium held on this position at the Univeristy of Aberdeen in 1972 had been summarized by the editors as follows: "Why does a woman go into labor at term? . . . What has become clear in recent years is that part, at least, of the signal that sets off labor comes from the fetus. In the nature of things such a fetal signal has to be endocrine in kind" (Klopper, A. and Gardner, J., *Endocrine Factors in Labour,* Cambridge University Press, London, 1973).

14. Treillis, "Sur une relation possible entre l'aire des tâches solaires et la positions des planètes." C.R.A.S. CCLXII (1966) 312.

15. Giorgio Piccardi, "Phénomènes astrophysiques et événements terrestres," lecture at the Palais de la Découverte, January 24, 1959.

16. Michel Gauquelin, *The Cosmic Clocks* (H. Regnery, Chicago, 1969) and *How Atmospheric Conditions Affect the Health* (Stein and Day, New York, 1972).

17. Let us mention the Fourth International Biometerological Congress, New Brunswick, Conn., 1966; Ninth Conference, Society for Biological Rhythm, Wiesbaden, Germany, 1967; Fourteenth and Fifteenth Convegno della Salute (Congress on Health), Ferrare, Italy; Second Symposium international sur les relations entre phénomènes solaires et terrestres en chimie physique et dans les sciences de la vie, Brussels, Belgium, 1968, and so on.

Conclusion

Is astrology illusion or reality? There are several possible answers. There is no doubt that in our world astrology is socially and psychologically very much alive. The horoscope is a product that is bought and sold, and that leads people to dreams. But the dreams of the clientele are answered by the deceptions of the charlatan, as well as by the illusions of the researcher who is sincere but not very lucid.

This psychological reality is based on a firmly rooted scientific error. As interesting as it may be, the origin of astrology was developed on mythological bases that are not at all compatible with modern scientific objectivity. And especially, serious scientific examination is never favorable to this ancient doctrine. Electronic astrology is no more than a gadget that has no solid basis at all; predictions about the future of the world are examples of rather pitiful Nostradamian sleight of hand. The horoscope is certainly a commercial reality, but it is a scientific illusion, or rather just an illusion.

But in spite of everything, is there not another possible end to the search for an astrological truth?

"No one ought to consider as unbelievable that a useful and healthy wisdom might emerge from astrological blasphemy and idiocy." Might this 400-year-old hope of the strange and genial Johannes Kepler be at the point of being realized in the second half of the twentieth century? It does not seem impossible. Recent discoveries have opened a new chapter in the interminable epic poem of astral beliefs. But they can hardly wear the compromising name of *astrology*. Besides, they propose a radical conceptual change in a problem that is as old as the world, one that until the present day has always been posed in irrational terms. A new sciene of the relationships between man and the cosmic factors has come to replace the ancient belief that has failed its task for so long.

The men of science who attempt to fill the void left by the practitioners of horoscopes wish to be as far away from popular astrology as possible. This is understandable: not simply because charlatans seek to profit from their work and to profit from public opinion; but also because the occultist necessarily speaks a different language than the scientist. The case is not unique in the history of science. The fortune teller and the explainer of dreams of days gone by have nothing in common with Freud's or Jung's interpretation of dreams.

There is no doubt that in a few cases some of the oneiric symbols of the old "dream books" cannot be completely stripped of every clinical truth. In the same way, it seems clear that the hour of birth seems a privileged moment in human life when certain still-mysterious cosmic influences can be manifested. That there might be a little more than simple chance in this fact is really impossible—and we have said so.

But this is an academic problem that only the historian of science will be able to answer later perhaps, if he possesses sufficient documentation. Today, the roller of charlatanism, disguised in the tinselled finery of modern technology, represents a psychological and social danger. And since the most painstaking studies have shown the inanity of horoscopes, there should be a strong rising up against this exploitation of public credulity. Unfaithful even to the cosmic dreams of antiquity and dangerous to the honest researcher, this exploitation dishonors those who practice it. This is why commercial astrology and its charlatans must be struggled against. But they need not be made into martyrs. The struggle must be carried on by revealing to the public the psychological traps of the horoscopes they buy, and by interesting them in the scientific work dedicated to cosmic influences. The sorcerer gave way to the doctor, even in the mind of the general public; at the dawn of the age of interplanetary travel, it is time that the fortune teller leave the stage in his turn, and be replaced by a new man of science.